The
FRIENDSHIP
FIX

The
FRIENDSHIP
FIX

The

Complete

Guide to Choosing,

Losing, and

Keeping Up

with

Your Friends

ANDREA BONIOR, PH.D.

Thomas Dunne Books
St. Martin's Griffin ♒ New York

THOMAS DUNNE BOOKS.

An imprint of St. Martin's Press.

THE FRIENDSHIP FIX. Copyright © 2011 by Andrea Bonior, Ph.D. Foreword copyright © 2011 by Abby Wilner. All rights reserved. Printed in the United States of America. For information, address St. Martin's Press, 175 Fifth Avenue, New York, N.Y. 10010.

www.thomasdunnebooks.com

www.stmartins.com

Title page illustration by Jamey Christoph

Library of Congress Cataloging-in-Publication Data

Bonior, Andrea.
    The friendship fix : the complete guide to choosing, losing, and
keeping up with your friends / Andrea Bonior ; foreword by Abby Wilner.
        p. cm.
    ISBN 978-0-312-60731-9
    1. Friendship.   I. Title.
    BF575.F66B663 2011
    158.2'5—dc22   2010043599

First Edition: April 2011

10   9   8   7   6   5   4   3   2   1

For Suzie
and my JE family, friends of a lifetime,
and in loving memory of
Mary Strong, who blazed the trail

Contents

- I Promise We Don't All Have White Beards: How Therapy
  Can Help

- Stories from the Heart of Friendship
- It's True: Friends Really Do Make You Happier, Healthier,
  and Perhaps Even Smarter and Richer!
- 4 Simple Things You Can Do Tomorrow (Or Tonight,
  If You're Feeling Gung-ho)
- Excuses to Nip in the Bud Right Now
- Don't Just Sit There; Go Out and Friend Away!

Acknowledgments

To everyone who shared their stories: This book would be nothing without you. Your courage, humor, and candor lit the way for me, and I can't thank you enough for that—and for letting me have fun with your pseudonyms!

A great many thanks to my savvy and supportive literary agent, Linda Konner, whose patience and belief in me were indispensable throughout this process. And it was an honor to work with my marvelous editor, Toni Plummer, fabulous publicity manager, Rachel Ekstrom, and the fantastic team at Thomas Dunne Books/St. Martin's Press. Much appreciation to Abby Wilner for her beautiful foreword and been-there-done-that wisdom. Crystal Patriarche is a PR goddess and godsend all in one. Holly J. Morris and the gang at Express got the ball rolling (literally, on the softball field, and for my career). Heidi Brown's encouragement and logistical support—and much, much valued friendship—always gave me a boost at exactly the right moment. And I couldn't be luckier than to be on the receiving end of Madeira James's unique Web design talents.

Kelly Gifford and the "Elite"—yes, the name's meant to be ironic, but you know who you are—are part focus group, part support group, awesome women all, and represent the very best of the new frontier of friendship. Elizabeth, Sarah, Sue, Nicole, Leah, Rose Michele, and Marci are great company and comprise my favorite book club in the world. Laura Gertz, one of the warmest people I've ever known, is a limitless source of ideas and enthusiasm. Kathy Chretian, fellow health care maven/writer/mommy: you are brilliant. And I'm similarly inspired by Sunny Gettinger—you'd be in the dedication were it not for the misfortune of being in Trumbull!

To my beyond-wonderful in-laws, Sybil, Luis, David, and Judy: your cheerleading and tireless help made it possible for an at-home-mom also to be an author. Thank you, times a thousand. My parents, John and Georgette, and siblings and siblings-in-law—Jeff, Greg, Julie, Brian, Stephen, Amanda, Roddy, and Cris—provided a steady stream of support (and food and drink)!

And Andy, the best friend for whom the words *best friend*—and even *soul mate*—are laughingly inadequate: I simply adore you. Vance, Alina, and Ruby: you fill my days with smiles and my life with meaning. And Vance and Alina, when you're old enough to read this book, thank *us* for how much ice cream you got on those nights I was working on it!

Foreword

After graduating from college, I was in for a shock: My bachelor's degree didn't seem to make me any more marketable for a job, and far from being financially independent, I was back at home living with my parents. It turned out this was a common experience, as I eventually documented in *Quarterlife Crisis,* the term for the awkward transition from school to working adulthood. Although the twentysomething years are often thought to be the easiest, most carefree time of one's life, this major life transition from perpetual student to working adult is more often accompanied by debt and stress than it is by glamorous parties or romantic dinners. In fact, the quarterlife years in one's twenties and thirties are accompanied by changes to and questions surrounding careers, relationships, and finances. Yet there is one aspect of the quarterlife crisis that is rarely discussed: the changing nature of friendships.

Friendships tend to happen naturally in school through the college years; it is easy to find friends with whom you have much in common. Yet once we enter the "real world," the friendship landscape becomes murky. The social boundaries between coworkers are less clear, and scheduling and geography don't allow for the same natural, comfortable pattern that became second nature in school. In fact, for many, friendships are the first priority in school.

Before we're adults, friends often seem more important than family and certainly come before homework and grades. Upon entering the "real world," however, we are faced with a myriad of new responsibilities, most notably the big *j-o-b* that takes up the majority of our waking hours. It can be harder to relate to friends when you no longer share the common ground of school, and when your workplaces and lifestyles can be so different. As additional priorities enter our life, they further complicate the friendship picture. Some friends get married, preferring quiet couples' nights to rowdy bar-hopping, while others stay in the singles scene. Then kids may enter the picture, even further deepening that rift and presenting boundaries that make what used to be simply hanging out a nearly impossible coordinated effort that requires more planning than a bridezilla's wedding.

Although friendships become more complicated during this transitional time, they are also more important. It's now taking longer than ever to become "adults" in the traditional sense. Our parents' model of adulthood is simply not a reality for most twenty-somethings. We are taking longer than ever to settle into a job, find the right partner, and become financially independent. We're in need of a surrogate family more than ever before as we navigate life's options and think about "settling" down.

As life changes, so do friendships. It's no longer easy to knock on someone's door, even call them, and just "hang out" without planning days or even weeks ahead of time. We have so many other priorities now, whether they are jobs, significant others, kids, or families. It seems like we've become busier and busier and always have some kind of errand to run that could take priority over getting together with a friend, but it's so important to maintain meaningful, lasting friendships—for our mental health, and for that bond no other relationship can provide.

We finally have a much-needed manual to help us understand

how to make and maintain friends as adults. Dr. Andrea Bonior has been providing witty words of wisdom to quarterlifers for years in her *Washington Post Express* column, and now with *The Friendship Fix*, she proves to be that voice of wisdom and comfort once again. The advice here is invaluable, no matter what stage of quarterlife you are in, and she tells it to you like a friend, without being condescending or preachy—and certainly with a full accounting of all the challenges going on in our lives as we attempt to build and maintain ever-important friendships.

—ABBY WILNER

The
FRIENDSHIP
FIX

INTRODUCTION

The Challenges of Modern Friendship

In my many years of seeing young adults for therapy, two major things have always stood out. Yes, one is that the bubble skirt does no one any favors, but the other—perhaps more germane to this book—is that relationships can simply make or break our daily lives. Now, to anyone who's devoted significant mental real estate to chick flicks, Match.com, or *Judge Joe Brown*, this will come as no surprise. But what's often overlooked is that the relationships that give us reason to wake up in the morning—and sometimes reason to duck, screaming, back under the covers—are not just the romantic ones. They're the platonic ones (which became romantic only that once, in 2005, when everyone was just way too friendly with Captain Morgan).

It is our friends who shape the course of our lives. Consider this: For all the people who are either monogamous or without partners (whom does that leave—Mario López?), romantic relationships make up just one, at most, of our companions, whereas friend relationships—and "friend" relationships—make up dozens, if not hundreds, of the people who matter most. From that snarky coworker who helps you get through Mondays, to that shopping partner you grew up with because your parents were fond of pinochle, to that confidante you've bared all with every week since Physics 101, they are the faces in our personal halls of fame.

Still, it's often assumed that finding a man, keeping a man, leaving a man, or even embalming a man is where the action is for young women. Why is this? Not only does this obviously exclude those who just don't go for men, but it also ignores the many people who went to see *Sex and the City* not for Big or Jimmy Choo, but for the four main characters—alone, together. Their friendship resonated. It mattered in a way that those of us who've relied on our friends as emotional life preservers completely understood. And we were willing to buy overpriced Jujyfruits and popcorn with the caloric equivalent of a hot fudge tanker in order to experience it on the big screen.

Now more than ever, more and more people are relying on their friends. With American women getting married later (a fond farewell to the notion of spinsterhood at twenty-five!) and more likely to put career before children even once they do get married, friends are becoming the new family. Women are starting to realize just how much those connections can mean—how much bliss they can create when they're fabulous and how much agony they can create when there's drama. And increasing numbers of young adults are spending their days texting, Tweeting, and collecting their friends online, making them real or virtual vacation mates, doctor's-office compatriots, and, of course, unwitting companions in the toilet stall.

But there's something very odd going on, and that's where my therapy experience comes in. Ask someone how they came up with their circle of best friends, and oftentimes they just fell into it, inadvertently and passively. Maybe the person was a roommate, a cubemate, or an aerobics mate. Such proximity can lead to wonderful relationships, but it is not sufficient in and of itself to the formation of a strong bond. Many people hope and expect to find soul mates romantically, but they often are more than willing to spend their entire twenties and thirties with a group of confidantes who are no more compatible with them than a bad toenail fungus. Why are expectations—and efforts—so low when it comes to choosing quality friendships? Why are there a million and one tips about how to go about scoring that first date, but the relationships we spend even more time with are sometimes fallen into at random?

Indeed, making supportive, lasting friendships can be even harder than dating, as many women in the trenches will tell you. (It's chapter 4, for those of you in need of instant gratification.) There are no standard courtship rituals for friend-making: no first-date protocols involving breath mints, skirt-length deliberation, or restaurant-choice analysis. When a man asks for a woman's number at a bar, the intent is clear, and it's not to compare notes on the stock market. When two work pals dance around the idea of hanging out after close of business, however, it can be much more ambiguous and awkward—there's not even a word for a platonic "date" equivalent in our language.

This book sets out to help you find your friendship soul mates. (Yes, *soul mates* plural. Luckily for all of us, the world of friendship—discounting those BFF lockets—is not a monogamous one.) It will also help you weather the storms inherent in any serious relationship, from jealousy and competition to growing apart, betrayal, and dealing with e-mail forwards that make you want to throw your laptop out the window. (*Snopes,* people!) Perhaps best of all, this book will do all the foregoing without once telling you what eyeliner to wear, the "it" jacket this season, or anything even remotely resembling "101 Sizzling Sex Secrets." For this, we can all be thankful.

1

FRIENDS

Who Needs 'Em?

There's an old adage about friends doubling your joy and cutting your sorrow in half. Unless I'm forgetting a part about whiskey, the point of this proverb is to remind us that friends serve important roles in our lives—profound, meaningful purposes that go much further than telling us if our butts look fat—and that their mere presence can have a phenomenal impact on our experience of happiness and pain.

HOW FRIENDS IMPROVE OUR HEALTH: WHAT YOUR GRANDMOTHER (AND A BUNCH OF DUDES IN WHITE LAB COATS) DISCOVERED

In fact, friendships have a host of emotional effects on us. Clinical depression, a disorder whose prevalence is growing sharply and whose typical age of onset—like (sadly) the market for thongs—is getting younger and younger, appears more likely to target those who feel unsupported by quality friendships. Anxiety disorders, from the phobia that makes a person go screaming when in the presence of mayonnaise to the debilitating and uncontrollable panic attacks that can confine someone to his or her house, are also associated with a lack of adequate social support.

The connection is especially true for one of the most extreme anxiety syndromes: posttraumatic stress disorder. Research shows that after suffering a trauma, whether it be a natural disaster, loss of a loved one, personal injury, accident, or assault, people with a higher level of social support in the form of friend and family relationships are much less likely to develop PTSD. We're not talking about friendships merely helping you whistle while you work: PTSD is a serious condition that, when left untreated, can lead to a lifetime of nightmares, terrors, an inability to engage in the normal daily routines of life, and not uncommonly, suicidal behavior.

Not only do solid relationships make us less likely to be afflicted with these and other psychological disorders, but they often make us more likely to recover from them quickly and smoothly if they do occur. Quality friendships can be both the apple and the antibiotic—a medley of prevention and cure.

Consider, also, the ways that friends themselves can encourage us to get proper health treatment. From the coworker who won't stop harping about that strange mole on our arm to the buddy who suffered from depression but shared the experience of how he got better, friends who have our best interests at heart can often push us in the direction of health. Certainly, for instance, if a loved one goes to therapy and extols its virtues, that destigmatization can do much more than any magazine ad ever could.

Friendships also affect our physical health in a more intangible way. Experiencing emotional intimacy in the form of positive relationships can help boost our immune system to better fight and heal from infection. As anyone who's tried to ignore a particularly bad itch most definitely knows, it can be virtually impossible to distinguish between mind and body. If that smells too much like patchouli for you, consider this: Social support has a significant effect on the prognosis of someone who has been diagnosed with HIV. We're talking about actual life spans here, affected directly by whether or not someone feels they have friends they can count on. Research upholds similar results for cancer, heart disease, and diabetes— and that's probably just the tip of the iceberg.

It's pretty amazing, really: all these physical and mental phenomena, determined in part by the simple idea of what we visualize when we think of our friendships. It sounds too simple. Just how is it that these relationships can do this?

There are quite a few ways. As therapists know, there is much to be gained from sharing your emotional experience with another person. Doing so can provide meaning, insight, and a sense of perspective that simply can't be gleaned from speaking into a mirror while wearing a disguise. (Believe me, I've tried.) People all over the world have learned that spilling their guts to another human being (even if, in the case of the Internet, that human being is pretending to be a twenty-five-year-old Catharine when he's really a forty-seven-year-old Roger) can have a magical effect. Why else would it be that often our automatic response, for better or for worse, when someone is going through pain is to say, *I know how you feel*? Is it really a surprise that one of the most affirming phrases in the English language (other than *Your car's engine is fine!*) is *I know what you mean*? Similarly, one of the most prized attributes that a woman tends to list in a man (even if she ignores that list and goes instead for the beer pong champion) is that he is a sensitive listener.

Indeed, people often describe profound relief when finding someone who can really hear what they're saying: it's validation to its highest power. The sense of euphoria that comes from connecting with another person who truly "gets" your experience—whether that experience involves growing up one of fourteen children or wanting to gag when smelling cilantro—can change one's life. People are prone to waxing poetic when they find it: it's the Church of Emotional Intimacy. They once were lost, and now they're found.

So many of our feelings can be made so much easier to manage, and perhaps more fun to experience, just by saying them aloud and letting them build a bridge between us and another person. Exposing our fears makes them much less frightening; affirming our triumphs makes them much more real; revealing our grief relieves us of carrying the burden completely alone. A compassionate and empathetic friend, much like a therapist, can give us and our emotions a foundation to cling to. It's the reason that merely having someone listen can be such a powerful experience, even if that person was secretly paying more attention to the cheerleaders at the halftime show. All jokes about therapists' fees aside, it is no shame that part of their ability to help lies in just being there, in the moment and attuned—those nods can be meaningful. A quality friend understands this and runs with it, knowing just how to validate their buddy's emotional state—whether that state stems from a hard-won personal triumph or just a particularly arduous commute home.

But another way that our platonic relationships wield such power is much more quantitative: Friends help us shape our identity. For all the emotional intangibles, they can also serve (like that infernal and unyielding doctor's scale) as a rather cold-blooded yardstick. Think of how often you view yourself—and even define your existence—through the "relativity perspective" of your friends, learning important clues about what you'll eventually believe yourself to be. I feel shorter around my taller friends, more outgoing among my wallflower ones, and, unfortunately, more gargoyle-esque around the ones who look like sitcom stars. This mosaic of comparisons shapes our core beliefs and often our self-esteem, and can help us figure out exactly where we stand in the world.

Perhaps this is one aspect of why the loss of a friendship can be so complex in the pain that it brings. It's not just that Sheila never returned our favorite cardigan. It's that we feel less funny, or less popular, or less knowledgeable of the ins and outs of *Lost* trivia when she, who was the audience that made us feel that way, is no longer there. Many people don't realize that the end of a meaningful friendship can literally signify the loss of a piece of their own identity. Such relationships can be the landscape background of our self-portraits; they provide the context of our traits, and when they disappear, those traits have no home. To paraphrase the old quandary, if a tree falls in the forest and there's no friend around to say, *That must've hurt!* does it still make a sound?

Friends themselves—especially that loudmouth Sarah you've known since she got banned from the slumber-party circuit—also give us even more direct feedback. Their reactions teach us what they appreciate about us, and they also are all too willing to let us know what we do that drives them up the wall. All these pieces of information, whether we like them or not, give us an enormous amount of insight into ourselves. We know we can be anal because our roommates used to resent our chore wheels; we know we sometimes interrupt because we notice others rolling their eyes; we know we're generous because we've heard our *amigas* extol the virtues of our cookie-gifting habit. It's our friends who give us daily feedback about the characteristics that make us who we are, and it's these assessments that stick with us when we define ourselves internally and externally. Life is full of constant pop quizzes about how we're doing as people, and often our friends are the only ones doing the grading. (And you thought your econ professor held a lot of power!)

There's also an incredibly profound and positive aspect of feeling that you're not alone. Existential psychologists have long known that fear of being and dying alone is one of our most primal anxieties, and it drives a host of human endeavors. Much of the world's greatest art, poetry, music, and storytelling (sorry, Tucker Max, you just missed the list) can be attributed on some level to our attempts to fight the angst of being by ourselves, literally and metaphorically. Human beings are born to connect with other people, and this need for affiliation is evident from our first infant clamors for a warm body to our later preference, confirmed for decades by social psychologists, for being in the presence of others when we are scared or anxious about something.

And the friendship gift, like the person who made too much fruitcake, just keeps on giving. Friendships also greatly increase the breadth of our interactions with the world around us. They might introduce us to a new philosophy, melody, perspective, or just a new thing to put in a pita. Of course, they might even be partly responsible for an addiction, an eating disorder, or a history of self-hatred. Therein lies their power. But when done right, they help us learn, they add laughter, and they further expand our world, giving it a depth that consists of anything from one more Italian restaurant to a lot fewer Saturday nights alone. On a grander scale, they can give us a whole new way of viewing the world.

Indeed, some of the habits we pick up from our friends are almost scary in their power. And we're not just talking about eating right from the peanut butter jar or overusing the phrase *train wreck*—friendships to some extent can determine our weight, our diets, our sleep habits, our levels of aggression and impatience, and our choices about smoking, drinking, and drug use. Experts who work on major public health campaigns are beginning to rely heavily on the fact that altering social norms—that is, how you expect your friends to behave—is one of the most direct routes to changing unhealthy habits. If your fellow carpooler of two years doesn't buckle her seat belt, chances are you will gradually be less likely to as well. If your circle of college friends never worried about safe sex, then I'm betting you weren't appearing in ads for Trojans. If your best girlfriend always blows her nose using the cover of a magazine, then chances are . . . (Okay, some habits are, thankfully, unlikely to gain additional followers.)

If friends are so influential, then what about friends' money? With a nod to the almighty dollar, it's no secret to those who work in advertising that peer pressure is king. And it's no surprise to anyone who's literally paid the price for a friend's expensive taste in pinot noir that who you hang out with has a major impact on your finances. Imagine how many levels of your monetary life your friends can affect: There's the obvious, like dragging you to bars and clubs whose cover charge could feed a pack of pubescent football players for a month. But then there's the less obvious, like the fact that friends help determine your standards about what kind of job you're willing to take, what kind of city you're willing to live in, and whether you consider living in a group house with a 1930s unrenovated bathroom an unacceptable example of "slumming it" or a downright artistic and jovial experience. Indeed, peer pressure, which tends to connote pimply preteens whose parents are on vacation, is far from absent in adulthood. Arguably, the fact that "grown-ups" have more spending money—as long as they didn't major in philosophy—means that your friends can have an even bigger effect on your bottom line.

In turn, our financial resources can then affect our physical and emotional health. From not having enough cash for that copay to being paralyzed with stress from living paycheck to paycheck (or, on the opposite end, being saddled with the guilt of having too much when so many have so little), the money we do or do not have can play an extremely large role in our fitness. And once again, it's friends who keep this cycle going.

Clearly, these attributes of friendship are so powerful that I no longer sound like a carnival huckster (or its modern equivalent, that overly polite e-mailer from Nigeria) when I say that friendship is associated with significant increases in psychological and physical health. More interesting still is that this is true even for "perceived" friendships: merely the idea of having friends can help someone get over a trauma more quickly and serve as a buffer against depression and anxiety.

Certainly, different people have different definitions of the word *friend*. Some people are downright overzealous with the term, bestowing it on everyone from the dude who suggested you switch to Verizon to the woman who twice rung you up at the Container Store. Others won't call you a friend unless you've twice posted bail. Surely there are pros and cons to each of these approaches, and the healthiest balance lies somewhere in between. Nonetheless, the science does back up that the perceptions of these connections matter.

And here's the kicker: overall, there's evidence that in the United States, we're identifying ourselves as having fewer and fewer friends. How can this be, with millions of people online literally collecting friends on social networking sites? If your average college student has enough Facebook friends to fill an Australian rugby league, why do we seem to be getting lonelier at the same time? Are "friends" as we know them losing their quality? Are we becoming the equivalent of what would have been called—in the days of poodle skirts and drive-in movies—friendship "tramps"?

BFF CULTURE: REPRESENTATIONS OF FRIENDSHIP IN CELEBRITY LAND

Certainly, there seems to be a cheapening of friendship in many aspects of pop culture. For every Carrie–Miranda–Samantha–Charlotte solid-gold bond, there's a set of starlets who are branded BFFs simply because they designed a line of nail polish together. Surely their destiny isn't really to be eating the early bird special together fifty years hence. (In fact, I'm betting instead it's to be brawling it out for the paparazzi, with or without underwear, in just a few flashbulb-filled months from now.)

Even the term *BFF* itself, when used for adults, was started sardonically, as a mocking takeoff on that overly optimistic promise scrawled in 1991 yearbooks everywhere—that we'd be Best Friends Forever. As grown-ups, we learned just how tall and naïve that order was: things would eventually get in the way. From incompatible homeroom schedules to arguments about the merits of Richard Marx, the odds were against those pairings lasting into one's golden years. We use *BFF* now all over the place, almost tongue in cheek, to refer to friendships ephemeral, superficial, even ridiculous—or so it started out. But here's the head-scratcher: many women have nothing but these high-flash, low-substance connections. The drama of their BFF breakups and makeups is actually the *foundation* of their platonic relationships. It's like a person who uses a vending machine for their three square meals a day—they're confusing junk for substance.

I'm pretty certain (even without Googling it!) that the changing ways we use technology have also had a profound impact on every aspect of our relationships. And this is undoubtedly part of the problem. Don't get me wrong: advances in computers and cell phones (we've come a long way since Pong!) have helped us immensely, and they've arguably done a great deal for friendships. But the technology appears to be growing faster than our ability to adapt to it; the social kinks appear more quickly than we can work them out. This means that we're using some of the old rules for new types of relationships, and some of the new manners (or lack thereof) for old, golden friendships. No wonder we're screwing up so many of them!

No doubt, different friendships serve different purposes. And not every one is meant to be profound or long lasting, though they all still have value. The woman who helped you get through that awful temp job was just not meant to become your maid of honor; that guy you count on for sarcastic fashion analysis would certainly be a poor choice to help you move. (Has he ever lifted anything other than a martini?) But no matter what exact way they fit into our lives, our friends' roles couldn't be more important to who we are. And the friendship problems that are so frequently experienced—the problems that I've spent years witnessing as a therapist, advice columnist, and professor of psychology (not to mention as, occasionally, a human)—can be downright toxic to our daily lives. I hear the worries all the time:

- I'm a grown woman, but I don't know how to make new, quality friendships.
- I just can't seem to trust anyone.
- I need to "break up" with a friend. Where the heck is my manual?
- I feel like I always give, and never get, in my relationships.
- I'm in a new school/city/job, and I can't seem to meet new friends. Please tell me I don't need to play softball!
- All my friends are in couples/getting married/having babies. How do I stop feeling like the odd one out?
- My friend betrayed me, and I can't stop hurting.
- I seem to have plenty of friends. So why do I feel so lonely?
- I want the best for my friend—so why am I always jealous of her?
- I'm bored and feel stalled in my friendships, and I can't figure out if it's them or me.
- I have real trouble opening up and showing the "real me" to people.
- This friendship is growing stale, but I can't figure out whether to let it go.
- I'm worried about a friend, but I don't know how to bring it up.
- My friend and I are always competing. Can this be a good thing?

- A friend hurt me, but I don't want to make her mad by confronting her.
- I can't seem to balance friendship and my classes/my boy-friend/my job/my Jack Russell terrier.
- I never know how to ask for help when I need it.
- I'm still wounded from a long-ago ex-friendship.

We've all been there. Some of us thousands of times, actually, if you count the vicarious experiences that are responsible for the wrinkles on my forehead. And whether you're male or female, single or coupled, fresh faced or battle worn, chances are there's been plenty of drama regarding one or more of these issues in your life. Most likely, that drama is only getting more intense, as we are spending more of our time and emotional energy with friends than ever before.

HOW FRIENDSHIP IS CHANGING IN THE AGE OF THE QUARTERLIFE CRISIS

This is especially true for young adults, who appear to be experiencing a longer adolescence than they did fifty years ago. No, it's not some miracle of hormonal science, but rather the advent of the quarterlife crisis. As much as some may scoff at that idea, the truth is that there are far fewer twenty-five-year-olds who are married and mortgaged now than there were when the Beatles—or even Duran Duran—ruled the airwaves. And while many people would consider this far from a crisis (especially those who can't commit to a wool coat, let alone a person), there appears to be a marked increase in aimlessness and discontent among those in this age group, especially when it comes to their lack of stability in careers and romantic relationships.

The reasons are varied: as college has gotten paradoxically more expensive and more necessary in order to make a living, it has become less typical to strike out on one's own and "settle" down by one's mid-twenties. Instead, those student loans might lead someone to bunk in Mom and Dad's basement until they've got a gray hair or two themselves. And while in the past it was one's spouse who tended to fill the role of confidant, dinner companion, and person to argue with over who screwed up the plane tickets, it is now much more likely to be one's friends. (Once again, the entrepreneurs are on the case: even the tiny vacation destination of Chincoteague, Virginia, boasts "his and hers" getaways for people who would rather kayak and drink wine with their friends than with their lovers.)

Perhaps most ironic, even weddings have grown to be extravagant celebrations of one's . . . friendships. They now make greeting cards to formalize the process of asking someone to be your bridesmaid; people broadcast the history of how they met the members of their wedding party in wedding programs and on wedding Web sites. Whole industries have been built around putting together bachelorette and bachelor parties, many of them entire weekends in exotic locales whose meticulous planning and spare-no-expense exuberance rival those of the honeymoon. Friends often shape the mood of the entire rehearsal dinner and wedding receptions, for better ("What a lovely toast, full of such sweet sentiment!") or for worse ("Is that your best man dirty dancing with Aunt Phyllis?").

Indeed, a young woman's number one man is much less likely to be a romantic partner now than he used to be. With the increasing role of coed friendships, many women do have a constant male companion—he just didn't happen to stand next to her in a tuxedo and wipe buttercream frosting from her face.

Clearly, friends are the new family. They can be the new bliss, the new laughter, the new meaning, and the new passion that give our lives purpose. They can also be the new migraine that's so bad we can't open our curtains. What separates the two scenarios is, at its most basic, the ability to choose good, healthy friendships and to get the most out of them.

So therein lies our task: to learn about what friends are good for us, and to figure out how to be good to them. To make sure that our friendships (with apologies to the U.S. Army) can help us be all that we can be.

Just how do we do this? Read on, my friends. (Yup, when it comes to defining the F-word itself, I'm one of the overzealous ones.)

2

WHAT KIND OF FRIEND ARE YOU? AND WHAT KIND IS RIGHT FOR YOU?

The Ancient Greeks said it best: Know thyself. And even though I don't think they were armed with Myers-Briggs personality tests, an on-call psychologist, or a library of self-help books, they might have been on to something.

"What makes a good friend?" I am often asked, but the reality is, the answer has different meanings for different people. Just as one person's dream date is another person's nightmare, or one person's perfect travel companion is someone who would send another person screaming back toward the airport, we all have different personality traits that determine what we look for in others. Nobody has the exact same list of what they bring to the friendship table, or what they're looking for once they're there. A good connection takes compatibility on both ends (sounds like an ad for a WiFi service!), and both sides must complement each other in particular ways.

Many people, especially women who've spent any time in a waiting room with a stack of magazines and chronically late doctors, believe they know the essence of their own true personalities. ARE YOU A PUSHOVER? or DO YOU COME ON TOO STRONG? the headlines scream at us, inviting us to find out other things such as whether or not we're a Man Stealer (Sample question: "Do you steal your friends' men?") or a Meal Moocher (Tell me: "Have you been known to mooch a meal?"). It shouldn't come as a shock to you that on many of these tests, we simply cheat. Our behavior is worthy of expulsion from the College of Self-Reflection or, at the very least, a meeting with the Academic Honor Council.

That's because we all tend to have ideas about who we are, and we tend to be confident in them—who could know us better than ourselves? So we want to see it reinforced in whatever magazine quiz or Facebook application we're using. Psychologists call this type of stacking the deck a self-fulfilling prophecy. But here's the problem: Many times we're wildly off base. We can never look at ourselves purely objectively. It's natural to view ourselves how we want to be seen, whether we have the motivation to be particularly flattering (*I know people don't tend to like me, but that's because they just can't handle how awesome I am*) or to berate ourselves (*She didn't call me back because I'm the biggest loser ever to have existed*). Your mirror can never be 100 percent accurate, especially if you consistently tend to look at things through either an *I rock!* or an *I suck!* lens. In other words, who we think we are and who our potential friends think we are are often entirely different concepts.

This makes it extremely important that we try to be more open-ended in the types of personality assessments that we do. Saying yes or no to some quickie questionnaire about our behaviors is not really going to get us anywhere, mainly because we're so prone to leading the witness, who in this case is the most important person in the whole trial.

So where can we start in assessing who we really are and, therefore, what we really might need in a friend? Think honestly, first of all, about your levels of extroversion and introversion. Oftentimes, this is a very misunderstood concept: People view extroverts as the ones who have the whole conference room in tears of laughter with their Lady Gaga impression. Or they're thought of as the Chatty Cathys who have totally spilled their guts to the barista by the time he makes their second Frappuccino. But merely being open or outgoing doesn't get to the heart of what extroversion is all about. Instead, as first envisioned by Carl Jung, it's about where you derive your energy. An extrovert can actually be a rather quiet and private person, just as an introvert can be the loudest blatherer on the subway. What matters most in assessing ourselves is to what extent being around other people is something that enlivens you, energizes you, or drains you.

Give some thought to how stimulated you are by new contacts with people. Even if you're not the initiator, are you generally enlivened by being around people, or drained? Imagine having a free day to fill with whatever you pleased. Are other people in that picture? Or is the thought of solitude much more rejuvenating? Does the idea of spending a long period of time with a large group of people—even if you like them—leave you wanting silence and Tylenol, or clamoring to schedule a repeat performance? If you've ever taken the Myers-Briggs Type Indicator (which is often given in career settings, or seen in some less legitimate versions floating around online), the first letter—*I* or *E*—indicates whether you tend more toward introversion or extroversion, respectively.

Most people aren't extreme in either direction, and everyone has times when they need to be alone. But giving some thought to your patterns can help you understand the larger role that friends may play in your day-to-day life, and how your interactions with them would best be suited.

WHAT TYPES OF PEOPLE SUIT YOU BEST?

It's also important to give some thought to the kind of characteristics that your friends need to have to fit best with you. Here are some considerations:

Do you need people to drag you out at night, or are you an initiator?

Or would you rather not be out at all?

How decisive are you when making plans? Does it drive you crazy to go back and forth and make last-minute changes, or are you always on the lookout to switch to a better option?

What do you consider your important values, and how rigid are you in them?

How sentimental are you? Are you big into birthdays, tokens of appreciation, or sweet notes for no reason? Do you cry at movies, or scoff at people who do so?

How much do you compartmentalize your life in terms of work and family?

Where's the line for humor in your world? The more outrageous, the better? Or do you think that oftentimes, people laugh at things that are inappropriate?

How private are you?

How physical are you? Do you like your friends to hug you or hang on you or fuss with your hair?

Are you looking for partners in crime? (Hopefully not for grand larceny, but do you view your friends' roles as to help you lose weight, find a man, take over your corporation?)

How adventurous are you? How spontaneous? How easily bored do you get, and how bothered by that are you?

Do you hold fast in your opinions, no matter what other people think?

Are you a doer or a thinker? Or both? Or neither?

How introspective are you?

How thin do you like to spread yourself? Do you like to have a huge gaggle of meaningful friendships, or just a few close ones?

Are you energized by differences of opinion, or do you often feel threatened or defensive when someone disagrees with you?

Do you tend to let your flaws hang out? Or do you prefer to keep up appearances?

How modest are you—physically, sexually? How much do you like to share?

Do you tend to be exacting about splitting bills, getting things back when borrowed, and so forth? Do you get annoyed when people aren't as conscientious as you?

Are you rigid about time frames?

Are plans with friends sacred, even if just informal agreements to hang out? Or have you been known to fade out at the last minute pretty often?

Do you like to be the center of attention?

What's your relationship to money?

How community focused are you?

How much of a do-gooder are you?

Do you love thinking through the ramifications of decisions, or do you like to choose something and stick to it?

How formal are you?

Do you hate feeling "lazy"?

How much of your daily life do you like to broadcast to the world?

Are you okay with your friends having different ideologies—religions, political affiliations—than you do?

Even though this list is not exhaustive, it probably feels exhausting! But the point is not for you to quantify yourself and develop some exact, numerical portrayal of what kind of person you are. It's to help highlight parts of yourself that you might not have thought about before, and how that might come across to other people.

When you meet a potential new friend, or you think about how well you're relating to the ones you currently have, these aspects of your makeup can help you assess how healthy the match is. They can point out obvious discrepancies between you and your friends, and also help you paint a picture of your "ideal" friend.

It might also give you a glimpse into places where you might be more likely to find meaningful friendships—say your adventurous spirit is being stifled, you might join a rock-climbing gym. Say you realize that you're being dragged out way too much when you'd rather be at home, then you might look for a cooking or crafting or film-buff organization, or for new connections online. It can also help this process to look analytically at how your best friendships have tended to develop in the past.

Learning from Successful Friendships

In regard to the friends you've had whom you've most enjoyed, think back to these questions:

- How did you meet them?
- Who made the first friendship "move," or did it happen much more passively?
- How different from you have they tended to be?
- How long did it take before the friendship reached its sweet spot?

Another exercise to help you prioritize the characteristics that most get to the heart of who you are is to think about how you would describe yourself in an ad on a platonic version of Match.com. (Don't worry—in this case, you need not shave off years or pounds from your vital stats.)

Seven words I'd use to describe myself are

_____   _____

_____   _____

_____   _____

_____

Seven words I'd use to describe the people I'd want to be my friends are

_____   _____

_____   _____

_____   _____

_____

PERSONALITY FACTORS IN FRIENDSHIP: DO OPPOSITES ATTRACT, OR ARE THEY DESTINED FOR *JUDGE JUDY?*

And here comes the conundrum: How similar do you want your friends to be to you? You may very well find that you want them to be like you in some ways—interests, morals, senses of humor—but could use some diversity in other ways—backgrounds, careers, levels of extroversion. Maybe you're a relatively shy person who's always enjoyed being around the life of the party; maybe you're a drama queen who likes to have a passive audience. Maybe you're a woman who enjoys hanging out more with guys; maybe you're a homebody who likes living vicariously through her adventurous friends. Or there might be the possibility that your best friends tend to be clones of you. The level of differences that you are comfortable with is another characteristic that will vary by person. Some people are bored by others who are too similar to them; some people are terrified by anyone who's not. Most people are somewhere in between—and it's up to you to figure out what works best.

In general, the better you are at developing relationships with people who are diverse from you, the richer and deeper the experiences you can have. It's up to you to ask yourself, Can this discrepancy be a connection-maker, or is it a dealbreaker?

IS IT A DEALBREAKER? DIFFERENCES IN . . .

The following are some of the most common differences that come up among friends. While some people wholeheartedly embrace these disparities, others find they can't. Be honest with yourself about what you can take and what you can't.

- Religion
- Politics
- Professional status
- Education
- Technological communication style (see chapter 3!)
- Health habits (smoking, drinking, drug use, eating, exercising habits)
- Financial resources
- Romantic relationship status
- Physical attractiveness (she's always hit on, you never are—or vice versa)

8 SIGNS A FRIENDSHIP IS WORKING

This poking and prodding shouldn't just be about new friendships; the ones you already have could benefit from some thought as well. Are they healthy? Are there trouble spots? Here are some clues:

1. You like who you are when you are around that person. You feel like your best self, and you act that way, too.

This is more than just "being yourself," which is overused and ambiguous enough that it can make someone be themselves all the way toward hitting their head against the wall. Instead, this is feeling that when you're relating to this person, the positive aspects of your personality are being brought out, and negative aspects—though not suppressed—have a much lower billing. It certainly doesn't mean that you present your life as a perfect masterpiece. It also doesn't preclude you from utilizing your friends for support while you show the sides of yourself that you consider to have flaws or weaknesses. (That's actually a role that friends can fill best.) But exposing those flaws should be for the greater purpose of feeling loved and even getting better. It should feel healthy, even if not completely comfortable. It's not that you're totally reveling in your "badness," but that you're getting validated by connecting with another person who really gets it, and loves you anyway.

This also means that you don't constantly do things you feel bad about with that friend: If you always get catty around Emily, or come off as a whiner, or feel lazy or boring or passive-aggressive, then it can be taken as a sign that something's not clicking right. Or if you're pushed into spending too much, drinking too much, or eating too little, that is a bad sign.

2. Overall, you are genuinely happy for positive things in your friend's life and genuinely bummed when things go wrong.

Of course you'll have twinges of jealousy when your friend scores that corner office; flawlessly achieves the effortless, happy pregnancy; or shows off her made-for-a-bikini body. (With all the Taco Bell she scarfs down, how is life fair?) But after those initial stings of envy wear off, you should come around and feel closer to her, not further away.

3. You find your friend interesting, and you feel like you both expand each other's horizons.

There is perhaps no greater sign of a friendship stagnation than total boredom between the two parties. This isn't to say that you're doomed if you absolutely cannot stomach hearing her repeat her mama drama for the umpteenth time. But here's the key: You should generally feel stimulated and interested in what she has to say. If after a six-month dry spell you can't think of a single thing she's said that you've cared to hear, then I'm hearing alarm bells going off in the background.

Good friendships also show an element of unpredictability. Not in crucial moments—like whether or not she'll actually show up to give you that ride after surgery—but in small sparks. Great friendships enjoy tiny, subtle surprises with new opinions, interesting stories, or a sudden urge for a new adventure. It keeps us on our toes and is the stuff that helps us grow. In a solid friendship, you'll have a general sense of the perspective that your friend might bring to the table, but you can't always predict it exactly, and he or she will surprise you in positive ways.

4. You look forward to spending time with him or her, but you don't feel so dependent on them that you can't function without some brief breaks in connectivity.

A good sign about your friendship is being excited to see a random text from that friend, letting you know that she just saw that guy from *Weeds* in the airport. A bad sign is that this is the thirty-seventh text she's sent you since lunch.

In this way, a true friendship is a bit like a romantic relationship: you want to miss the person when you haven't seen them in a while, but you don't want to be unable to go about your day without them holding your hand.

5. You feel like your friend knows the real you, or at least an approximation thereof, and that you know a similar level about them.

It's a rare friendship where self-disclosure is completely equal. The world is made up of a spectrum of undersharers and oversharers (and then there are the uber-oversharers!). But when the difference gets too off-balance, it's hard to keep a friendship from veering off-kilter. If you've got an intricate problem, it can be difficult to trust the advice of someone about whom you know so little that you're not really sure where their perspective is coming from. On the other hand, how uncomfortable would it be to trust someone whose life you know so well that you can make an Excel spreadsheet of all the different times she's contradicted herself, or the times her own advice has failed her?

6. Being together feels informal, not overly structured or forced.

It's natural to have first-date-like jitters at the beginning of a new friendship. (Will she notice the mustard on my sleeve? Worse yet, will she think it's bird poop?) But in a solid friendship, this abates over time, and conversation flows naturally and unself-consciously.

Of course, some people feel self-conscious around even their oldest, dearest friends. This is not necessarily a condemnation of all their friendships (unless they have particularly awful luck!) but more a sign that they need to do some work on themselves. Some people are more formal than others, and will never put their feet up on your sofa, even for an 11 P.M. popcorn-riddled viewing of *Gossip Girl*. But there's a difference between formality and anxiety. If you never seem to be able to feel comfortable with your friends, if you are always doubting yourself or are overly concerned about how you're coming across, it's time to think about exploring that pattern further.

7. There is a level of trust and reciprocity, a balance that no longer feels like tit for tat.

Trust is one of those most unquantifiable yet crucial elements of any deep friendship; without it, things can crash and burn quickly. But there's no way to force it, or even to guide it in a step-by-step matter. (Trust me—here's the least effective phrase of all time: *trust me!*)

But you'll usually know when trust isn't there, or you're reminded of it with a bit of nausea when you need to rely on that friend for something. As a general rule, friends shouldn't be the things in your life that are leading to gastrointestinal distress.

As for the reciprocity piece, this is crucial. It's that interesting dance that occurs when the relationship starts to grow not only in trust, but in interdependence and commitment as well. The first stages of friendships are often marked by a constant consciousness of reciprocity. ("He paid for parking this time; I'll do it next.") But over time, in healthy relationships, the reciprocity becomes more general and occurs more naturally. "Tit for tat" is no longer the MO of relationships that grow deeper and longer-term. Think of the type of friends whom you'd be comfortable asking to pick you up at the airport in an emergency when your original transportation falls through. Chances are that's a much smaller subset than whom you generally consider to be your friends. This is because, of course, it's an inherently unbalanced situation in that moment—they are giving you something you are not immediately repaying (other than regaling them with the riveting stories of your takeoff turbulence). And except for those of us who are total freeloaders, we can be comfortable doing this only with very good friends. In these relationships, we know there'll be a time at some point when we can do another as-yet-unknown favor for them, and no one needs to keep tally.

That's not to say, of course, that you won't buy them lunch on the way back from the airport to show appreciation for their effort. But you're not going to mark down exactly how much they spent for gas. Over time, the closer we get to people, the more inherent and automatic the reciprocity, the more we sail into—with the right people—a sort of equilibrium where we simply trust that we'll each be there for the other, and we stop keeping score.

The absence of this, over time, can be a strain. When that balance gets out of whack, so begins the drama.

8. You admire this person, but you can also relate to them.

This balance can be precarious. Just like the person who's dating someone that they feel is "out of their league," when you think that your friend deserves someone better than you, or that they're doing you a favor by hanging out, that dynamic is bound to lead to disaster. Putting a friend up on a pedestal means that it will be difficult for you to show your real self to them, and it will be hard for you to be realistic when they need help with their own vulnerabilities. Feeling unworthy every time you see her kick-ass apartment or her five thousand advanced degrees is not exactly conducive to your personal growth.

Of course, you shouldn't be afraid to "aim high" in whom you aspire to hang out with. Variety is the spice of life, friendships included. But if there's something about the dynamic between the two of you that makes you feel like chopped liver, you've got to figure out how to get past that if your friendship hopes to stand the test of time.

And being a kiss-up does no favors to your friend, either. If you are the person who is pedestal-ized, you're probably feeling uncomfortable in your own right. As much as it may feel good to have some admiration, there's something unnerving about feeling like someone can't handle the "real" you. You're probably dying to give them the reality check that the real you can't sing a note, can't parallel park, or that you have a tendency to chew your toenails and spit them into that cup above the drawer where you keep your sports bras.

So, if most of your close friendships meet these eight criteria, you're doing something right, or you've been blessed with the luck of a relationship lotto winner. Now it's time to think about strengthening those relationships even further, perhaps adding some additional ones and weathering the inevitable bumps in the road. We'll learn about all those things in the upcoming chapters.

If few or none of your friendships seem to match these snapshots, then usually there are three possibilities of what's going on. You might be picking not-so-wonderful companions as friends, you might not be doing your part to keep those friendships strong, or there might be something getting in the way of your ability to connect and engage in friendships. We'll discuss how to work through these issues later on. For now, it's important that for a good friendship, you at least know it when you see it.

You'll notice that all these principles are somewhat general. Nowhere in there are dictums about how much you should work out together or whether or not they should love your purple pants. It's important to recognize that no two relationships are the same, and you actually need several different types of personalities—and friendship dynamics—in order to have a nice variety.

ONE SIZE WON'T FIT ALL: MAKING ROOM FOR DIFFERENT STYLES IN YOUR FRIENDSHIP REPERTOIRE

The older we get, and the more splintered our lives become, the harder it can be to keep up meaningful emotional intimacy and interactions with our friends. But there's a plus side, too, in that we have more freedom to have different friendships that fill different needs in our lives. No longer are we the terrified teenager who put all her emotional eggs in that one person's BFF basket. The richer our lives become, the more life experiences we have; and the more layers we develop in personality and interests, the more room there is for different types of friendships.

Everyone has a different blend of friends and friendships within their collection. The key is to realize that most likely no one friend can provide us, as adults, absolutely everything that we need. And to avoid the drama of disappointment, we must realize that some types of friends, while great for some things, can have their limitations. See what I mean below, with some friend types you might recognize all too well:

The Perennial Cheerleader

She might not have the actual pompons, but she's got the spirit (How 'bout You?). She's on some sort of happy juice, or else something's wrong with her eyes, because she never can see the glass as anything but half full. And she'll be the first to let you know that.

Good for: Telling you how muscular your upper arms are; assuring you that "it will be okay and he'll forget about it tomorrow" when your boss walked in on you painting your toenails; never losing faith that you'll ace that test, get that job, find that soul mate or even just a good deal on a new purse.

Not so great for: Giving you an honest assessment of why you might need to work on your interpersonal skills, your financial habits, or your discipline. Letting you really vent and occasionally dwell on your misery after a bad breakup or a bad bout of food poisoning. Validating your negative feelings.

The Go-To Guy

Gay or straight, he's always good for providing a male perspective and having the ability to laugh and not judge when you're less than "ladylike." He'll gladly be your date at your third cousin's wedding, and if you're lucky, he might even help you pick up the sofa you bought on Craigslist.

Good for: Giving a perspective that might—just maybe—be a little bit different because of that Y chromosome. Not tending to fall into the same types of drama that can occasionally infect all-female friendships.

Not so great for: Fitting in seamlessly at a get-together for chick flicks. Totally getting your experiences as a woman in a man's world.

The Character

On days when we're feeling less kind, we'd call her a drama queen. She's always got a story, and each time it's simply the "craziest thing that's ever happened." A routine phone call can easily turn into you giving her advice on three different dilemmas that have popped up since this afternoon.

Good for: Making you appreciate all that goes smoothly in your own life. Flexing your advice-giving muscles. Entertainment.

Not so good for: Just chilling out. Being there for you without distraction. Having a normal, ho-hum outing—or conversation—when you're exhausted or zoned out.

The Den Mother

She's all her name implies and more; sometimes she even feels like a hall monitor or a chaperone.

Good for: Bringing you soup when you're sick. Making sure that your plants get watered when you're gone. Having an extra toothbrush for you when you want to crash at her place.

Not so great for: Letting your grammar mistakes go by unnoticed. Letting her hair down with you when you need to blow off some steam. Making you certain she means it when she claims she's not judging you for that one-night stand.

The Always-Up-for-It Girl

Want to head out to that happy hour tomorrow night? Check. Want to take that road trip to the hot springs? Check. Want to stalk that house on Fourteenth Street to see if that's really where the cast of *The Real World* is living? Check, check, check.

Good for: Being your companion when the bars are closed and all your other friends have gone to bed. Telling you that trekking Everest without a lick of proper training is a viable possibility. Being willing to compete in that annual wasabi-eating contest.

Not so great for: Sitting down and chilling out. Sticking to mundane commitments when something more exciting comes along. Being willing to deal with the day-in, day-out grind that can come from being roommates. Letting you nap when traveling together.

The Overanalyzer

A talker and a thinker, this person has conversations with you that would be taxing to transcribe. Incredibly smart, she can nonetheless wear you out.

Good for: Plowing energetically into the second hour of "what if?" discussions about your job possibilities. Decoding the nuance of the ambiguous text message that that dude left after your second date. Miraculously flinging a six-page e-mail into your in-box exactly when you need some procrastination.

Not so great for: Giving you a simple yes or no about Thai or Chinese food. Leaving you feeling good about your decision to choose a job over grad school, or the elopement over the fairy-tale wedding.

The Party Animal

You've never seen this girl wearing anything other than a tube top, and you're not sure what her real eyelashes look like. Or maybe it's a guy who always carries with him the permanent look of the smoky bars or beer pong tournaments he's just been hanging out in.

Good for: The excitement of being out and about. Making you feel young (until you're hungover the next morning). Giving you stories to laugh about later.

Not so good for: Helping you develop healthy habits or think through something introspectively. Contributing to your resolution to budget, eat, or sleep better.

The Professional Mentor

When all your other friends still don't seem to actually understand what it is that you *do,* this friend has at least one foot in your field—or did at one time—and gets where you're going and what you'd like to be. She's someone you look up to and whose guidance you'd give the weight of the world, but there's a formality there that you don't think will—or should—ever go away.

Good for: Having the most valuable opinion of all about whether you should apply for that position in another department. Giving you a reality check about whether your salary is up to snuff. Getting you the name—and e-mail address—of the person who can help you sort out your security-clearance paperwork.

Not so great for: Bearing witness to your emotional breakdown about your boss. Listening to your off-color joke about rodents.

The Passive Listener

You never jabber on as much as you do with the Passive Listener. You find yourself somehow telling her about your first-grade nemesis, or you suddenly realize that she knows more than your mother does about your history of scoliosis. Eye-rolling, checking her watch, and sighing in boredom are foreign concepts to her—she's great. Yet you barely seem to know anything about her.

Good for: Isn't it obvious? You could tell her anything, man!

Not so great for: Giving you definitive advice. Giving you a chance to help *her.* Making you feel like you really, really know what's going on inside her head.

The Social Director

The Social Director is the center of every gathering, the insider for every event. She'll also take every interaction on as her pet project. Have your eye on that guy at the end of the bar? She's spoken to him and gotten him to come over while you went to the bathroom. Disappointed that your clam chowder didn't come with extra bread? She's got the waiter apologizing—and toting a new baguette— within seconds.

Good for: Giving the scoop about that new bistro, getting you tickets to U2, knowing exactly what you're talking about when you cite some weird trend in martinis. Being the glue that mixes everyone together at your awkward, ill-planned barbecue. Getting you in touch with someone who has lived in the city you're visiting and can actually answer your question about whether that hiking trail allows dogs.

Not so great for: Making you feel like her one-and-only. Giving you her full attention while you're on the phone—or even eating dinner—together. Giving you a sense of certainty that your secrets are in a vault.

The Opinionator

This one's got her mind made up. You know exactly where she stands on the next election, your neighborhood's garbage pickup schedule, and whether or not you should get bangs again. And she's not going to let you hear the end of it.

Good for: Making you over, telling you how you should organize your freezer, knowing a much better place for you to get your nails done.

Not so good for: Making you feel good when you've put on a few pounds. Enduring your indecisiveness about whether to bring your new boyfriend to Thanksgiving. Telling you the white lie that your awful haircut won't cause traffic accidents.

The Specific-Event Filler

Unlike most of the other types of friendships, this friend fills a very particular purpose, and you really can't imagine doing other things with her. Maybe you always shop together, or you have a standing date for getting highlights done. Or maybe she's your gym buddy, but you really can't picture it ever progressing to more than that.

Good for: Whatever it is that you do! Providing structure and predictability in your life. Giving you company when you'd rather not be alone.

Not so good for: Taking the friendship to another level. These friendships are sometimes comfortable but stagnant, lacking the emotional intimacy that makes them truly profound.

Of course, your closest-of-the-close friends will defy being categorized because you know them so well, they could never fit into a box. Nonetheless, the second tier of friendship has quite a lot of room for an entire cast of characters. And before we start hoping that one person can give us everything, it's important to note how much we can get—and how much we can't—from the various people assembled therein.

THE FRENEMY: WHAT THE HECK IS IT, AND WHY WOULD I WANT ONE?

Recently, with our cultural love for portmanteaus (the many permutations of *Bennifer*, anyone?), frenemies have come to the public's attention. Usually, a frenemy is someone with whom you have a rather love–hate relationship, someone who dances on that line between friend and foe. There are several different types of these relationships. A frenemy can be any of the following:

- In the style of "Keep your friends close, but keep your enemies closer," someone whom you play nice with, but only in order to keep tabs on and not let screw you over.
- Someone with whom you used to be good friends, but a betrayal or a prolonged competition has added a dynamic

to your relationship where you don't really have each other's best interests at heart.

- Someone whom you've never really liked but have decided to keep up appearances with for the path of least resistance. (You run in the same social circle, work at the same office, live in the same building, have families that are friends with each other, and so forth.)

Is it worth it to keep these relationships going? In any of these three situations, it can be, though you'll generally do better the closer you can approach authenticity. While it's fine to chitchat with a frenemy at some crowded party, don't make her your bridesmaid or let her visit you in the hospital. She's bound to add more stress than she takes away.

On the opposite end of the frenemy spectrum is the platonic crush. Sometimes the spark of admiration we have for someone in a friendly way can pack nearly the wallop of a romantic infatuation. You're excited to spend time with them; you respect them immensely; you try to be on your best behavior around them. Many a legendary friendship has begun this way. But like romantic infatuations, the relationship eventually needs to come down to earth in order for it to survive. Otherwise, you run into the dreaded imbalance of power.

It can sometimes seem, with all these criteria, that we're on the lookout for perfect people. But if you think about it, if we picked only perfect people as friends, who'd be picking us? Nonetheless, it's an important question: Where do you draw the line between accepting and embracing someone for who they are and deciding they're not good enough for you? If you think that someone has a lot of growing up to do, should you ever stick it out to enjoy the ride? Can you honestly be in a friendship with someone whose flaws are part of the dynamic? The answer can be surprising.

Says Jade:

The more I think about Bethany, the more I'm really glad we're friends. We're in grad school together and I'm interested to see how she grows as a person. She was always someone who wants what she wants when she wants it. She's brilliant: by the time she was in eighth grade, she was taking calculus.

But she also really, really needs validation from the opposite sex. She needs to be pretty, desired, and wanted, and she had a thing for teachers and coaches. That's how she met her ex-husband. She got married at seventeen, had three kids within only a few years. So now she's twenty-two. And she cheated on her husband, and even though he wanted to get back together, she couldn't/wouldn't stop the affair.

Looking back (I'm thirty-three), I remember being that age, and a lot changed between twenty-one and twenty-five, and even more between twenty-five and thirty. She hasn't even reached the first big change. I feel really good that she doesn't feel that she needs to lie to me. I made it very clear to her—your life is your own. I might not agree with what you do, but I'm not going to hate you for it, unless you, like, kill my dog.

In the span of knowing her a couple of years, I've seen her going through an evolution. . . . She's learning more that there are consequences to her actions. It's nice to see that— she's growing up! I see a lot of myself in her, and at some point, I grew up. Seeing it happen, I'm proud. She really can think about people other than herself.

We meet for breakfast weekly. I have to think that me being so straightforward to her is helpful. I'll tell her when she's being obnoxious. I think no one has ever called her out on behaving badly. I feel like I'm serving that role. She's never had girlfriends; she's had girls that she knows, or the wives of her husband's friends, but I think I'm probably her first real girlfriend.

I keep growing more affection for her. She still has moments where she's a little flaky. But to me, her flaws are just the price of admission. And she's on the brink of becoming not such a bad person. Is she ever going to be Mother Teresa? No. But at least she's not going to be a selfish little wench anymore. I think it's healthy for her to have a friend like me who says it like it is.

Clearly, Jade is getting something out of this relationship. The question becomes Where do you draw the line? It's important to realize that you shouldn't have to get to the point of serving as your friend's therapist.

And for all these friendships that have their place despite their flaws, there are plenty of stories of friendships going bad because—let's face it—friendships can go really, really bad. This book will help you identify the red flags warning of that. But as an initial cautionary tale, I offer you the following, from Maria:

I had become good friends with Katie through work. We started going out at night. The second time we went out, this guy was hitting on me. She liked his friend, but the friend didn't like her back, so she gets pissed off at me—saying it's my fault. She starts yelling at the guy who was talking to me, calling him an asshole. I'm like, *Thanks for ruining that!* That should have been a red flag.

But this stuff would happen, and it really got on my nerves. But she would call and apologize the next day: "I'm so sorry, I was drunk. I totally overreacted."

Out with her again another time, she blows up, same kind of story, and can't stop screaming at me. At some point in the cab home, she starts crying, saying, "I don't know why I was even born. I'm the worst person in the world." I tell her not to worry about it, that I'm still her friend, that she just overreacted. And the next day at work, I get a card saying how lucky she is to be friends with me, and can I ever forgive her? I said I thought we needed a break.

We went probably seven months without talking. She got a boyfriend. I didn't even know until I got an e-mail from her, saying, "I'm so in love. He's the greatest guy in the world." But then, of course, they break up, and my phone is blowing up with texts and calls from her. "Please go out with me! I'm miserable!" I get sucked in again, ending up with her drunk and throwing up on my couch, and the next morning unable to drive herself the forty minutes home because she doesn't know where her contact lenses are. My other friends say, "You've got to cut it off!"

But the next day she e-mails, "I'm the worst person ever, the worst friend, no guys want me, there's no point in living anymore, I'm such a bad person. I can't even face the day anymore."

So of course, I write her a letter back, saying, "I know things look bad now, but you're going to find another guy. Take it day by day, see the light; you deserve somebody better, I'm always here for you. Don't think you don't have anyone to talk to."

So she'd call me, every night, talking for hours about this awful, horrible, mistreating guy. Then she wrote me another letter: "I don't want to hear crap from you. I'm going back to him. I don't care what any of you think." Then she dropped me again for another month.

Three days ago, I got another phone call from her. "He

broke up with me. When can we hang out?" I've finally reached the point where I'm like, *I'm too old for this.*

Maria had the signs from the get-go; the main reason she got so entangled was she felt guilty and kept getting sucked in. She wanted to be a good person and, of course, you should not ignore a friend's talk of severe hopelessness or anything that hints at suicidality. But by the time Maria had gotten to that point, her friend had enmeshed her much more than was good for Maria. In this case, the only thing that will truly help Katie is to get professional help. While a friend can and should do the urging toward that, they can't be the help themselves, and should never be expected to be.

Ultimately, it's much easier to avoid getting entangled than it is to break the connection later on, as Maria found out. But even that is easier said than done. Read on for a look at the ways that technology has made this process even harder.

3

OH, THE TECHNOLOGY!

*How Facebook, MySpace, Twitter, Blogs, and
Text Messaging Are Changing
Who Is Near and Who Is Dear*

Once upon a time, when two people were interested in talking with each other, they picked up the phone. If that time was particularly ancient, then that "phone" was made of rocks, banana leaves, or woolly mammoth dung, and perhaps didn't offer much in the way of fiberoptics. But even more recently—when Bruce Willis was already on the big screen but still had hair—people had landline phones as the sole way to communicate instantly across distances. In short, the phone was the extent of the action.

Of course, nothing about that communication was really "instant," as compared to now. To start, people could make calls only from select places—usually consisting of their homes, their offices, or those mysterious phone booths that were also good for dudes with horn-rimmed glasses to don their capes. People simply had no expectation that if they had a thought while they were driving across a bridge, they'd be able to share it with their friend Shirley right that very second. Or that if they called Marge and Marge didn't answer, they'd even be able to leave her a message instead of trying again later. (I mean really, can you imagine? Not being able to leave messages for people? The hardship defies comprehension.)

Now, of course, things couldn't be more different. Even voice mail itself feels ancient. A large percentage of younger adults appear to ignore it altogether in favor of texting. You might notice this phenomenon—you might even be part of it if you never bother to listen to voice mails; you just pay more attention to whose calls you missed. This is fine if both people are playing by the same rules, but don't forget that your Aunt JoAnne has no idea you never bothered to listen to what she was inviting you to or asking you about.

Phones themselves have developed serious problems with attention spans. First the touch tone made the dialing faster, then the answering machine gave you no way to be unreachable, even while you were out, and then the phones themselves, and phone service, got ubiquitous—we now get offended if we don't get a cell signal while scaling Mount Kilimanjaro. Dialing gave way to pushing buttons, which then gave way to texting. (There are now three times as many text messages sent as mobile phone calls made, according to Nielsen research. And one wonders if a single one of them would be recognizable—in grammar, spelling, and punctuation—to our old friend Shirley!)

Texting—sort of the love child between calling and e-mailing—is short, but it's not always so sweet. Unlike face-to-face communication or even e-mail, texting lets us place something—immediately—into someone else's consciousness, whether they want it there, and are adequately prepared to deal with it right at that moment, or not. For some friendships, especially those that are long distance and already suffering from a lack of face time, this access can lend a hand with emotional intimacy. The Thursday-afternoon *Just thinking of you!* texts can be a blessing. But in other friendships, for all that texting adds, it also can taketh away.

First, there are many nuances that are missing in text messages as compared to the spoken, or even e-mailed, word. *Congratulations!*—even with sixteen exclamation points—isn't quite the same when it comes on a screen, devoid of a happy voice's high-pitched tone or the sound of dancing a jig in the background. Similarly, something meant to be good-natured ribbing can fall flat via text and sound cruelly serious. It's arguable that the more we rely only on digital communication in our relationships, the less rich and deep these communications become.

Think about the friends you text most often. What do you usually say? Is the immediacy and lack of face time a benefit (*Running late; go ahead and order the California rolls*) or a liability (*I just slept with your brother*)? Is texting taking away from the quality of your relationship and preventing a real back-and-forth dialogue when that dialogue is sorely needed? When's the last time that you sat down, face-to-face? Can your latest news really be all that great when it's spelled *gr8*?

There's an even more sinister side of texting. While we are busy sending, receiving, and overanalyzing texts from others, we are also busy not paying attention to those who exist in front of us. While a quick *Happy Birthday* text to a friend across the country can arguably help improve our relationship with that friend, what about the fact that we're sending that text while we're supposed to be connecting with a new coworker? Are we really with the people that we're with when our thumbs are tappity-tapping against a keypad and our brains are being mildly amused by the fact that our phone autocorrected *Andy* to be spelled as *Body*?

No doubt this is a generational issue. The older you are, the less likely you are to rely on texting in your relationships, and the more likely you are to be sorely aware of all that texting seems to be lacking. But even younger people (for whom Bruce Willis never had hair) can sometimes see how texting can cut them off from the world right in front of their face. Sometimes, in an effort to connect to several people at once, they are oddly not really connected anywhere.

While many people talk about how texting has "replaced" the phone call, there's something else at play as well. Often, people text when they would never have bothered to make a phone call in the first place. This theoretically has a positive side—you can keep the host updated about running late without disrupting the party; you can send a quick comment to someone about your thoughts on the movie you just saw without worrying about interrupting that person's dinner. But the interesting thing is, it probably is interrupting the party or the dinner, in an even larger way. This is because the checking and the waiting for those text messages to arrive—and the scurrying to look at your phone when you hear one—has become a compulsion for many people. The landline phone might not be interrupting the party like fifteen years ago, but the host may be so glued to their BlackBerry that they were never really engaging in anything that could be interrupted in the first place. Everything is already flightier and more superficial; one can even picture people standing in the corner fiddling with their phones instead of dipping into the spinach appetizer.

What causes this? Why is it so easy to get hooked on a cell phone at the expense of the potential of flesh-and-blood interactions a few yards away? There's something curious about our brains that makes us desperate to keep checking these devices, to keep feeling "connected" to the world. The thrill of the chase—and the expectation of an e-mail or a text—can sometimes be far more stimulating than the communication itself. (Research by Brian Knutson, a Stanford neuroscientist, has consistently shown that the brain gets more lit up with activity when anticipating a reward than when actually receiving it.) Hoping that new friend will text you is enough to keep you eyeing your phone all day, even if her text will be nothing particularly special.

And so we stay tethered to our machines, thinking we're connecting when we might be nothing but disconnected from the world around us. And yet the quality of those connections—the real meaning of our texting relationships—is the part that makes or breaks our happiness. Sometimes the electronic connections leave a lot to be desired, to put it mildly.

It's remarkable that all these technological intricacies were barely a dot on the friendship landscape fifteen years ago. Instant messaging—yet another technological advance that will make the eyes of anyone who doesn't trust computers glaze over—has also changed dynamics directly. Like texting, but with computers, instant messaging or "chatting" online has the unique trait of keeping a conversation "open" for hours, like carrying a walkie-talkie. It offers continued contact for coworkers who want to quickly and effortlessly volley a question to the other side of the office and get an immediate response, but the coworkers receiving those messages might bristle at the interruption. Also, it provides a lasting record of how an exact conversation went down. That permanence—and potential loss of privacy—is not something to be taken lightly, and it's one of the many ways that IM is *not* just like talking (unless you are used to your friends wearing a tape recorder all the time).

THE DIFFERENCE BETWEEN "FRIENDING" AND BEFRIENDING

An even bigger storm has been brewing, of course, and it's called social networking. Though twenty years ago, the phrase *social networking* would have referred to a gathering of accountants with business cards and some extra chips and dip, now its meaning is all about technology. Web sites that connect people through their profiles and their agreements to be connected with one another have been proliferating for a decade or so, but only in the past couple of years have they truly exploded to the point that your godmother knows about them. Facebook, which at press time appears to have become the behemoth of them all, has so saturated popular culture and social relationships that it's been the subject of dozens of front-page articles in old-fashioned newspapers.

A gap has grown between the adopters of social networking sites and the ones who steadfastly refuse to participate in them. Both sides have their arguments—"It's the wave of the future; it helps me keep in contact with people I'd otherwise lose touch with" versus "I prefer my friends live and in person. If they want to talk to me, they should just pick up the phone." And both these sets of arguments have inherent flaws. The ones who rejoice in social networking's ability to keep them in contact with all kinds of people often forget that some of those connections are tenuous at best, and there's no real connecting going on other than seeing that person's tiny little name and photo icon on their screen every once in a while. At the same time, those who resist social networking because they think someone should just pick up the phone and call are ignoring the fact that at one time, the phone itself was thought of in the same wary, suspicious way that online communication is now. ("Why call when you can come by and visit?") Honestly, that type of resistance might have less to do with principles and more to do with the arbitrary contexts of when and where they happened to be born and what they are comfortable with.

Indeed, these sites are growing, and it's probably less prudent to ignore them altogether than to learn how to use them responsibly, healthily, and for maximum benefit. After all, the number of dilemmas that can arise when navigating these friendships is astronomical.

The first quandary of social networking depends on how old you were when you got involved with it. For millions of late twenty- and thirtysomethings, getting on Facebook or Twitter or MySpace or other sites has been not just about connecting but also about reconnecting. It's been about rediscovering that long-lost friend from middle school who, when you last saw her, was despondent that Keanu Reeves's rock band never took off. It's about showing people from your past how far you've come and how those old yearbook entries proved right—what a long, strange trip it's been.

But for younger folks, who've been on these sites since they had braces, the reconnection angle is not so prevalent. That's because there was never a disconnect in the first place. It sounds wonderful to be able to keep in touch so effortlessly. After all, it used to be that a cross-country move spelled doom for a high school friendship. Who wouldn't want that to be less of a barrier? But there's a darker side to all this connectivity. Specifically, how do you ever change, grow, or take risks when you have the constant watchful eye of a gallery of people who've been following you since you had that wardrobe malfunction at the swimming pool?

How can you reinvent yourself—or even just make a few changes—when someone is watching your every move?

One antidote to this problem is awareness of the issue itself. It can be quite dangerous when the basic human tendency to conform mixes with the increasing lack of privacy that online social networking brings. So be aware of the threat, and don't be afraid to get some space every once in a while. Whether it's by privacy settings or (gasp!) not putting every aspect of your thoughts and feelings online, you need to remember that you have the right to do things without a live studio audience (and the laugh track that it can bring). The need for privacy and space as we experiment with a new career path, a new outlook on life, or even a new way of cutting our bangs is losing out to our constant need to have the validation of everyone around us. In reality, that bad haircut actually helps us grow. Choosing at first the wrong major, boyfriend, or apartment can actually be a beneficial stepping stone toward independence, insight, and growth. But when we constantly look to others to decide things (Facebook status poll: *What should I have for lunch today?*) we are denying ourselves a valuable opportunity. We must not let the connections that have been sustaining us become the tethers that strangle us or force us to be forever what others believe we're supposed to be.

Even for the generations of people who didn't suffer from the problem of constant connectivity, and whose forays into social networking Web sites are actually about reconnecting after having lost touch, sometimes what actually constitutes a true connection can be downright murky. In fact, sometimes "friending"—when the *friending* is in quotes—is not like befriending at all.

Exhibit *A*: One morning I thought about an old high school friend I hadn't seen in eight or nine years. I found myself wondering what she was up to, remembering how fun she was, imagining how nice it would be to reconnect. This went on for several minutes, until my mind wandered a bit more and I realized that I actually *had* reconnected with her on Facebook in a flurry of late-night and overexuberant friend requests made a few months before. We had exchanged the typical initial back-and-forth messages—expressing unbelievable excitement to have found each other, looking enthusiastically at each other's "gorgeous" and "awesome" photos and travels, gushing at each other's new lives and jobs and families. And sadly, it somehow hadn't sunk in to me at all. I have no doubt that if I had actually gotten together with her, and talked face-to-face about all the very same things even briefly, then there's no way I would have forgotten. Such a meeting would've been imbued with so much more meaning, and would have been so much more of a real connection, had I actually heard her laugh or seen her in all three dimensions across from me. Instead, our "reconnection" was, in truth, no more than words and images on a laptop screen—a screen that shared space with a knitting blog, a work assignment, and a tzatziki recipe. I was horrified.

But this lies at the heart of this friendship conundrum. Do these fleeting interactions online ("I work for Netflix now!!!" "I ate there once—it was great!" "Hey—I'm LOL at that video!") even register in our brains in nearly the same way as an oral conversation would?

Do our hearts really process a reunion when it comes without eye contact, a hug, or even the sound of someone's voice?

It's important to keep this in mind whenever we're initiating new friendships or reconnecting online. Especially when people first join a social networking Web site, there's often an overactive flurry (in a way that's probably not unlike mainlining heroin) of collecting friends, new and old. But here's the rub: Collecting is just that— collecting. It is most certainly not always connecting. Actually, sometimes the initial joy of reconnecting with a long-lost close friend can turn downright sad when it seems that all the friend wanted was just a quick peek into your social networking profile without the real experience of reconnecting. Though, of course, it's understandable to be curious about what people are up to and just want to swoop in and briefly find out, it's important you don't leave someone hanging when they were a big part of your life. Case in point, from Sadie, a thirtysomething attorney:

> Marie and I were best friends in elementary school—you know, the kind joined at the hip—and then went to different middle schools and high schools, but we stayed in touch for a good long while. Like many, we eventually fell out of touch. I was a holdout when it came to Facebook, but finally joined long after most of my friends. I got in contact with many former classmates, among others. I found Marie and sent her a friend request, which she accepted. I was so excited to reconnect and find out what she was up to! So I wrote a little note on her Wall about how happy I was to have found her and asking her what was new in her life. Well, I never heard anything, and I was so heartbroken. I just wanted a little hello, and that would have made me perfectly happy. I don't see her post very much, so perhaps she is one of those people

who just aren't into Facebook or has moved on to more interesting things. I did check recently, and she didn't defriend me or anything like that, so I'm trying not to take it too personally. But—it would have been really neat to find out where she is in life and maybe even have met up again eventually.

Here's a tip: Every time you reconnect with someone online, make an effort to actually process that person's meaning to you—not as a data file, but as a human being. Give a little more intense attention to their messages as you try to actually visualize some of the memories you're tossing around, and let yourself really chuckle when you're busy typing "LOL." Try not to overuse the same phrases over and over again with different people about how wonderful it is to reconnect. Talk specifics. And make the immediacy work for you, not against you: If you happen to have a pleasant memory that hits you at some point during the day with this person, drop them a quick line to make the connection—it's so much more meaningful than just another link that they probably won't ever click on, or a generic marveling about how much time has passed. Make an honest effort to run into that person in the flesh if you're in the same area, rather than just giving it lip service while secretly thinking you'd have no way to fit it in. (After all, you've got to reserve your evenings for "reconnecting" via the Internet with the next person in line!)

Some people, however, thrive with the distance created by the Internet. "Why can I be such good 'friends' with someone on a message board or Facebook—but not in 'real' life?" asks Dara, a twenty-nine-year-old. "Is it just the medium itself that allows me to participate actively—since it's not as much work? Is there some comfort in the computer barrier even though it's not anonymous in those forums that I do most often? Weird."

Online communities that develop because of common interests can often take on a life of their own. Message boards, where people post responses to topic categories (threads) and questions and comments in real time, can become extremely close-knit communities, even when no one in the group has met "in real life" (IRL). Whether you are a fan of sleuthing out mysteries, retiling your bathroom, or planning your wedding, there is an online message board for you, and it doesn't take long for topics to get personal.

It's an interesting paradox: Someone online, and several states away, might know your daily thoughts, see pictures of your bedroom, your kids, and your vacations, and even hear about a pregnancy or a death in the family before your "real life" friends or loved ones do. In these environments, people are often dancing back and forth between distance and intimacy. You may never have met these people in person, yet you "chat" with them constantly each day. And often that might make them the first to know your news, even if they won't be joining you for an in-person drink afterwards.

Other aspects of message board life feel *all too much* like real life, if real life were all junior high school. Message board drama has become a fact of life for entire swaths of Web-savvy people. Stories like the following from Ellie are not uncommon:

> I joined a private message board that was a spinoff of a board on a corporate Web site. Caitlin was not well liked on the original board, but a bunch of us who hated the drama and felt bad for her asked her to come to the private board. Well, she only proved to be exactly what the women who picked on her knew her to be. This girl was awful. The biggest drama stemmed from someone critiquing some photos she had taken and posted, saying that the pictures she had taken on this newer shoot were not as good as the ones she had taken in a past shoot. She had asked for opinions! She fired back at

the woman who said that, whom she had prior issues with, and was really, really nasty to her. I was so offended by her comments that, stupidly, I got involved, and that did it. She started typing things like, "I know you all want me to leave, but I am not going anywhere. You will never be able to get rid of me, even if you delete me from the board." She did the same thing about a month later on another message board, and had done it on the original board a year prior. It's apparently her MO.

When I eventually left to get away from her, she found me on Facebook. She would reply to mutual friends' posts with nonsense. I probably would not have cared, except it was almost like being stalked. When I had last spoken to her, she essentially told me, "You think people like you, but they really don't." She thought it was funny that she had hurt other people on the board. It really stressed me out for a long time. The whole thing was miserable and scary.

Indeed, sometimes the anonymous people behind a computer screen miles away from yours can have bigger effects on your psyche than you'd ever imagine. A particularly unique take on this comes from well-known bloggers, who cultivate readers that might technically be strangers, but feel like anything but.

Wendy Bernard, founder of the immensely popular blog *Knit and Tonic* and author of two knitting books, talks about how she handles the occasionally strange dynamics that can develop between bloggers and their readers:

I don't edit comments. And I've had only one or two really blatant and stupid comments that are just so bad, I'll leave them there and let the other readers pile on and protect me. The readers have your back. Which, some days, feels creepy—

that people could be so interested in me—but then again, it's really nice.

This blog is this entity inside my head and my heart, and I don't want it to be nasty. And if I start reading things that are negative that other people say about me on other blogs, it would freak me out, so I don't.

When I get rude e-mails, I write a nice e-mail back. I'll write a draft e-mail ripping them to shreds, but I never send it. I just pretend, to defuse it. But out of all my supportive comments, if I get one that's not supportive, my heart sinks. I don't want to hurt people's feelings. I don't want to piss people off. But people often come off sounding more angry than they really are, and it's so easy for me to jump to a conclusion, so when I write them back, and they write back, I think maybe they weren't all that mad after all.

The thing about having a blog: It becomes an entity of your own personality, and you're affected by what's there. It almost feels like a living, breathing thing. It's like you have to figure out a coping strategy for this part of your life. If you go on vacation and you don't write for a while, you feel guilty. This whole social aspect of it is really interesting. I don't know how I'll ever end it.

A funny story: I guess I had been writing about getting a new couch. Fast-forward awhile, and I'm on the set of a knitting TV show, in the green room. There were three other ladies preparing for the segment; we're all quietly knitting. Somebody says, "Are you Wendy from *Knit and Tonic*?"

I say, "Yes."

"How's it going?" the woman says.

"Good!"

"How are your pattern sales going?"

"Oh, really well! I saved up enough to get a new computer!"

"But I thought you were going to get a couch!"

I was blown away. I didn't know how closely that person had read the blog; we were just having a lazy conversation among strangers, and she had known all these details of my life without my knowing.

The thing is, I've never shown a picture of my husband or where I live. But I do write a lot of stuff that's very personal, and I don't remember it, since I don't go back and read it. So when things like that happen, it's very odd. I have people who pay a little bit too close attention. They think I'm their "friend." But what is it, really?

Jenny Lawson, aka the Bloggess to her blog readers and huge number of Twitter followers, discusses the occasional tension between her "real" life and her online life, and how that affects some of her relationships:

There have definitely been issues. I now let all my real-life friends know that if they don't want something Tweeted about, they have to clarify that immediately. I probably should draw up some sort of waiver. For me, friends on Twitter don't really feel like true friends until I know something personal about them. I have a lot of readers who suffer from anxiety or depression, and they direct-message me because they know I've been through it as well. Those are the people I usually keep up with the most because we share a personal connection.

I have a lot of online friends that I'm closer to than people I know in real life. I think having someone to "talk to" online who doesn't know you in real life can be immensely freeing. There are no expectations, and you are able to confide in someone who you know won't turn around and tell all your coworkers how much you want to strangle them. What's odd to me is how I can become very close to someone online and then when they decide to quit Twitter or blogging, I miss them. I miss someone I never actually met. It's a strange feeling.

I have a lot of different online personas, although deep down, they're all me. I have a sweet mommy blog and a satirical sex blog, a snarky advice column, and an offensive personal blog, plus the Twitter account that's filled with bizarre non sequiturs and threats of violence. In real life, I can be sweet as honey while yelling out the C-word in a crowded room, and online I'm the same way. It's just easier to see that division online. I think we're all a little complicated, but I don't expect everyone to love every aspect of my personality. My grandparents, for example, tend to pretend that my mommy blog is the only blog that actually exists. And really, that's fine because I don't think I could write as freely on my personal blog, knowing my sweet granny would be reading about sex later.

Sometimes I'll call to catch up with friends and relatives, and I'll find myself either offended that they don't already know what's going on with me because they don't follow me online, or pissed off because they do read me and so every time I try to talk, they stop me because they've already read it. It probably sucks to be my friend in real life. I might owe a lot of people apologies!

Indeed, the Internet itself sometimes can intensify, inflame, and manipulate emotions. It's easy to see this not just in friend relationships, but also in misunderstood e-mails between colleagues, or increasingly heated comment threads on Web sites. Often, anonymity is a catalyst toward revealing overly personal information or fanning the flames of overly emotional topics. Unfortunately, all too often, civility is lost. I'm not recommending that we all don satin gloves and speak the Queen's English whenever we fire up our browsers, but I do think it's important to evaluate constantly what our motives are when we start to lay on the snark. There's not yet enough research about the kinds of vengeful and angry interactions that often escalate online, but we can start by asking ourselves when we find ourselves getting carried away in negativity, What are we really getting out of this? Do we really feel better after doing this? Is it truly improving or enriching our health or our lives? Is it teaching us anything? Or is it like abusing a substance—giving us a brief bit of tension relief, making us feel better to escape the aspects of our lives that we are not fond of but, in the meantime, doing nothing to solve those problems or let us really connect with someone who cares and can help?

It's easy to get preachy on this topic. And who has not been tempted to add their own thirty-seven cents onto a critical diatribe against some celebrity or politician's seemingly inane quote (which may or may not have been taken totally out of context)? It's all too easy to succumb to a very negative force. And the more desensitized we get to the cruelty, the harder the shells around us become and the less capable we are of truly connecting with others and reaping all the best benefits of friendship. Without this real connection and empathy, we're just helping each other corrode.

But there can also be a positive side to the anonymity of the Internet. People suffering from debilitating ailments can often find solace in support groups online, where the relief of not having to make eye contact or explain why your apartment is such a mess can add to a tangible level of comfort. When someone's life has been rocked by a devastating diagnosis, or a staggering loss, or even just an unusual predicament rare enough that no one else seems to understand, it can be immensely helpful to find a sounding board among people who know a bit about what you're going through but who will never even know your full name. In this case, anonymity doesn't hinder a real connection from developing; it actually lays the foundation for it.

At other times, the anonymity can do nothing but create distance. And this is true even when it's not related to snarking or trolling or any of the other techno-words that would send your great aunt into a tizzy of confusion. Whenever an online relationship grows, whether it be between people on a message board, bloggers and their commenters, Twitterers and their followers, or friends of friends on Facebook, a fundamental question lies uneasily beneath the surface: Who really *is* this person?

Many times, this question is eventually answered face-to-face or phone-to-phone with the chuckling acknowledgment that someone is much shorter, or louder, or paler, or Long Island–accented, than was initially expected after getting to know them online. And the relationship carries on, having been given the added dimension of in-person connectivity and touch. But other times, the answer doesn't turn out quite so well. Every now and then, your friend Emily is not Emily at all, but rather a hirsute middle-aged man named Fred. You may scoff, but it happens: Countless cases exist of people becoming beloved on message boards, blogs, and Web sites only to be found out later to be completely fabricating entire aspects of their existence. Some people are after money, others notoriety, still others sympathy, attention, or love. But the ability to instantly doctor photos, effortlessly plagiarize other people's words, or quickly gather a following of hundreds without any of them ever having seen you in the light of day has given rise to many, many scams where a "friend"—even after years of daily online contact—was found out to be nothing of the sort.

What do you really know about your friends? Reality check: Before you bare all, or extend your generosity with a click of a PayPal donation, or with detailed accounts of your sympathy or even a link to someone's story, ask yourself if there's a chance that your connection to this person is part illusion. Be honest about whether whatever emotions you're feeling—outrage, sadness, utter joy— might be clouding your judgment. Ask yourself whether, if this person approached you as a stranger at a gas station, you'd think their request was equally inspiring or a total joke.

We can never be too careful about the amount of information we share online. Much has been written about how social networking, blogging, and Tweeting have led to a redefinition—or even an all-out bulldozing—of the notions of privacy. Some people are so used to sharing their intimate details that they don't even give the process an initial thought, let alone second ones. But think—and rethink—you must!

Should I Share It Online?

Whenever you choose to share something particularly personal in what is actually a public space (yes, public: there's absolutely some pimply preteen hacker who can find your latest blog entry, no matter what your settings are), ask yourself these questions:

- Why am I sharing this? What do I really hope to get from it? Are my motivations healthy?
- Are there people who would read this and change their opinion of me? How would that affect me? Might this be insensitive to them or others? Might it be hurtful or confusing? Is this really a representation of who I am?
- Will this get in the way of other goals (professional, financial, emotional, logistical)?
- Am I comfortable with this piece of information being, for all intents and purposes, public and permanent? Can I foresee a time when I might change my views on this topic and not want an electronic relic around?

Certainly, not all online friending of old real-life friends, or the development of new ones, is shallow or dangerous. Social networking Web sites have truly rekindled some friendships that otherwise would've melted away forever. And there is something to be said for these sites themselves helping to strengthen those connections on a daily basis, as your old friend comments on your latest news, laughs (or at least claims they did!) at the latest video you posted, or helps you realize that you both know the same Tricia.

But here's another catch: The really substantial online reconnections are more likely to happen with people who spend the most time on these sites. And the more time someone spends on Facebook, or MySpace, or Twitter, or whatever social networking Web site sprouted last week, long after the old-fashioned paper version of this book went to press, the more "friends" that person tends to have on these Web sites. And you see where this is going: The more friends the person has on the sites, the thinner they tend to spread themselves. And the question of quantity versus quality comes into play all over again. They might comment to you a lot, but if you're one of a thousand people they do that with, your meaning in their lives is harder to figure.

Another tip: If there's someone you really want to reconnect with, don't forget the beauty of a letter, even in digital form. Send an e-mail (gasp!)—even one that's a few paragraphs long. A constant stream of one-line comments can go only so far. Ask a question to get a real dialogue going, rather than just providing a wham-bam commentary. Your online circle will consider itself strengthened.

TO FRIEND OR NOT TO FRIEND: DRAWING (AND KEEPING!) BOUNDARIES IN YOUR TECHNO-CIRCLE

And whom should you actually let in that circle? It's the conundrum virtually everyone has dealt with: A friend request is staring at you, leaving you uncertain or even a bit queasy. Sometimes the issue is whether to make the request yourself, or whether to give Facebook a clue that yes, indeed, you do know that person they keep suggesting that you do. *Should I friend this person or not friend this person? Will I regret it later?*

Will I hurt their feelings, or make them think I'm in love with them, or totally over them? Will I be bombarded by a series of 9,876 game requests that make me wish we'd never had that chance meeting in biology class?

If you are ever going to stay on task about valuing quality over quantity, you've got to do an honest assessment with each request. Certainly, some people have reason to be friending every Tom, Dick, and Harry (or Emily, Caitlyn, and Brendan) out there because they've chosen to make social networking sites their main means of self-promotion or business marketing. But for most of us who want to keep some semblance of a correlation between friending and befriending, there are some things to consider.

TO FRIEND OR NOT TO FRIEND

An ex. Are you with someone now? How would that person feel about your friending this person? Is this person with someone? How would you feel about seeing him or her with someone? How long were you together, and how did this relationship end? Is it easier to establish a general policy, or decide on a case-by-case basis? How many mutual friends do you have? Can you use some privacy controls? Would you be okay with this person making reference to your past relationship? Do you realistically want anything more to do with this person? Does he or she realistically want anything more to do with you, or are you just a number? Will they be the type of "friend" to stay in the woodwork, or will they inundate your every status update with annoying commentary?

A work "friend." Do you really want this person seeing how much work time you spend on Facebook? Would you benefit from a clearer division between your personal and professional life? (Read more about this in chapter 5.) With all professional contacts, try to assess whether they seem to want to reserve the social networking Web sites just for their personal life. On Facebook, for instance, members are allowed to post what connections they are interested in. If your coworker seems to be using it only as a dating site, then clearly it might be awkward for you to be sniffing around in his profile. But if someone lists "networking" as one of the things they are after, you'll know that most likely, you'd be welcome.

A work supervisor. Generally, you shouldn't take the initiative to friend a work supervisor unless your office is so close and collegial that you are certain it would be well received. If they friend you, it might be awkward not to accept their request. Once again, you need to remember your privacy options, so that your boss isn't privy to the photos of you at that bachelorette party.

A professional acquaintance. Again, social networking Web sites can be gold mines for traditional networking. But make sure that person appears to be on the same page as you in their desire for this. And bear in mind that if they have access to all your online friends, there can be complications that develop with friend "poaching" or competition.

A friendship that you're trying to phase out. If you're trying to move away from a friendship, friending them on a social networking site could become a spark that will keep that friendship going longer than you'd like.

A family member. Do you tend to reveal things that might be confusing or embarrassing to people in your family? Would they cramp your style? What is the balance of power in your relationship, and might you always feel like they're "checking up" on you? Can this add to your ability to keep in touch in a positive way, or might it become a burden?

An old frenemy or competitor. What are you really after? Are you spying or looking for one-upmanship? Are you willing to mend fences? Who wants this more—them or you?

An old unrequited crush. Are you in a relationship now? Will this person make you feel inferior or embarrassed? Are you actually hoping to reconnect in a romantic way and deluding yourself? Are you prepared for this person to say something you don't like? Might you be prone to a preoccupation with looking at their profile (or, ahem!, cyberstalking them)?

A person I don't know. It serves as a useful commentary on our peculiar society (and the need for this book—hey, want another copy?) that deciding whether to confirm as a "friend" someone we wouldn't be able to pick out of a police lineup is a regular activity. These mysterious frienders tend to fall into several categories:

- People we've forgotten from long ago
- People who are trying to market themselves to us
- Friends of friends who clearly remember us more than we remember them
- Friends of friends who have decided to try to friend all their friends' friends (say that three times fast!), in the hope of a universal singing of "Kumbaya," or the ability to invite four thousand people to their hair salon opening
- People who are trying to get our credit card number, steal our identity, and make our lives a living hell

Obviously, trying to figure out the person's motives for the friending and determining whether or not you are on board with being part of that plan is the most important factor. Are you comfortable with being just a number?

A garden-variety acquaintance. Don't friend this person just to up your friend number; friend them only if you're genuinely interested in staying in contact with them, and perhaps growing the relationship further.

All these complexities—and the impersonal and instant nature of online communications and connections—can greatly affect even "real life" relationships that have existed for some time. As the definitions of *friend* on social networking sites become even more varied and confusing, more people are looking to streamline and make their own rules. ("From now on, I'll cull anybody whose last name I can't spell." "From this point forward, I'll do a monthly sweep of people with whom my only contact in the last year has been to deny their request that I join Farkle.") When people do this, they might choose to defriend whole swaths of people at a time. There's also individual defriending, where maybe after feeling slighted by someone, the injured party takes the easier route (clicking a red *X* in a box) rather than the more uncomfortable one (confronting you about the slight over brunch). Or maybe someone's just fed up with seeing your thirtieth "Looking forward to the weekend!" status message.

Either way, it's a strange thing to encounter: being defriended. And sometimes, due to the peculiar nature of social networking and having so many friends that you don't exactly have them all memorized, you might only know that some mysterious person has done it if you suddenly notice the number diminish by one. You may even be online as it happens, sending you into a maelstrom of emotions when you know that someone has defriended you at that very moment. Kate, a thirty-two-year-old blogger, explains these very feelings:

My first response was anger. What loser just defriended me?
Next came hurt feelings. Do I write too many stupid status

updates? Did I offend someone? I realized it was slightly ridiculous, but still, I felt the need to identify the perp. I became obsessed with discovering who it was. I started with a friend-profiling approach, trying to think of the most obscurely connected Facebook friends I had—like the guy I thought was someone else when I accepted his friend request—progressing to such would-be-Facebook dissers as ex-boyfriends and others I didn't know all that well. (This did highlight how many random "friends" I've accumulated.) When this failed, I methodically scrolled through each friend in order to try to detect a noticeable absence. This was completely useless. Apparently, whoever it was was not that important in my life. Still, I felt this obsession. Otherwise, this dis would be completely one-sided, and I would not let my frenemy win on that level, either. At one point during my search, I told my husband, "When I find out who it is, they'll be sorry they ever friended me!" And he said, "They apparently already are."

We laughed over that. I could totally see that my reaction was absurd and it really shouldn't be that big of a deal. But this felt different from a real-life snub, since at least in real life, you know who is doing the snubbing. Of course, some of this is my sensitivity talking. If this happened to my husband, he would not have taken it personally. A few days later, I figured out who it was. It dawned on me that I was no longer receiving multiple not-funny-but-trying-too-hard-to-be status updates from one of my (former) Facebook friends. This was a guy whom I barely knew and who had friended me in the first place! So. Lame. He was actually one of the most annoying people I was Facebook friends with, so I suppose he did both of us a favor in the end. Or at least me. But it could have been handled better by Lame Man had he just sent me a little pre-dis message like, "Hey! You're super-cool, but I feel like we have different interests." That he chose to just silently (cowardly) defriend me for whatever reason left a bad taste in my mouth.

But I think dealing with this has helped me accept that defriending happens and it's not so big of a deal. I mean, my friend list is so full of randoms that it's to be expected. And just because I'm supertolerant of people hanging on as my Facebook friend despite me getting zero out of the cyber-connection doesn't mean that everyone else is, too. I'm more respecting of that. Theoretically.

One way to counteract this problem is not to keep such a close eye on your friend or follower numbers on social networking sites. Not only will this help prevent you even noticing if someone relatively inconsequential in your life decides to give you the online ax, but it also can prevent you from becoming preoccupied with the number itself, like a Casanova counting his conquests. If you're concerned only with upping your total, you're losing sight of the real reason these connections exist. (Of course, if you are on a social networking site solely to promote your business, that is a different story. But then again, none of this friendship advice would apply to you. And stop spamming me!)

Additionally, to counteract the uneasiness that comes from being defriended, try to turn the situation into a positive opportunity. Do a reality check. Be realistic about what you would really have gotten out of "keeping" that "friend"—maybe even your own standards and rules need to be reevaluated. Just don't get so enthusiastic in your own prunings that you put someone else in that same awkward position without sensitivity to their plight. Defriending is okay—but not in a hot-button, reactionary way. Give yourself a waiting period. (Yes, the type of thing that is required for divorces and gun ownership can also come in handy for pulling the friend-ship trigger.)

A FEW MORE COMMANDMENTS OF
SOCiAL NETWORKiNG

Just when you thought you had it down, there are a few more ways to butcher your friendships on Facebook:

Thou shalt not spill someone else's beans. It's easy to forget that when you post something on someone's online profile, their entire network may have access to it. Thus, never comment on their news unless it's actually already been posted on that very site. Maybe she hasn't told her family she's pregnant; maybe none of his coworkers know that he's job-searching. And remember that not everyone on her friend list was invited to her wedding, so don't make mention of how beautiful the invitation was, unless you're purposely trying to flaunt your status of making the cut in front of those who did not. (And why would you do that?)

Thou shalt not be passive-aggressive. Don't use a vague status message or Tweet to make someone ask you what's wrong. While it may occasionally work, a continued pattern of this can become habit and make you less practiced in having those difficult conversations healthily. Begging someone for attention, through a cryptic post or vaguely angry song lyrics, is not fair to the person you're trying to send a message to, and it will make you come across as annoyingly vague or melodramatic to everyone else.

Thou shalt not try to cover all bases all the time; otherwise, what are you really saying? One of the perils of having a friend list that's huge and heterogeneous (everyone from your second cousin to your old boss to the guy you've had three dates with is on there!) is that you might often feel the need to try to please everyone at the same time.

While a nice impulse, it often takes away all authenticity. Tweets such as "Annie is sooo excited to go to the beach with her ladies this weekend, but sooo bummed to have to miss Julie's baby shower because of it!" sound just ridiculous. Julie isn't meant to know that you're going to be having a blast at the beach, and your sun-and-fun girlfriends don't have a dire need to know you're upset about what you're missing while you're with them. An approach that tries to please everyone gets so watered down, it doesn't really say anything at all.

Thou shalt use privacy controls! It's amazing that more people don't utilize the privacy controls all these sites have. Explore them. Realize that your mother doesn't have to see all your photos, and your coworkers don't have to see all the posts on your Wall. You can block strangers from even seeing you at all. Take advantage of these possibilities, and you'll sleep better at night.

SIGNS YOU MAY BE ADDICTED TO ONLINE CONNECTION

It's important to know when you might be spending too much time "connected," as in connected to a wireless signal instead of to the real aspects of life that sustain you. Here's a list of red flags:

You keep spending more time online while your in-person relationships are declining or deteriorating.

You are nervous, edgy, or preoccupied with thoughts about getting online when you are away from your online connection.

Your school performance, job, or finances are suffering because of the amount of time you spend online.

You are losing a significant amount of sleep for your online activity.

You find yourself having difficulty setting—or sticking to—limits about how much time you spend on the computer.

You find yourself lying to others, engaging in deceit (for
instance, using different screen names), or trying to cover
the tracks of how much time you spend online.

You use getting online as a pick-me-up, constantly and ha-
bitually expecting it to change your mood.

When you get online after an uncomfortable time away, you
feel a surge of relief, followed by a sense of guilt.

If several of these signs describe you, you very well might have
a problem with spending too much time online. The emerging treat-
ments for these issues are beyond the scope of this book, but there
is help, in the form of cognitive-behavioral therapy and even some
support groups.

The next wave of the Internet, according to people who can
use the word *terabyte* more convincingly in a sentence than I can,
may very well be to help increase real-world connections. For some
people, this might not be their goal for all their online relationships. As we mentioned, some seem to gain intimacy and comfort
with the boundaries of the monitor screen. But with other relationships, the technology is best used as a stepping stone toward
the more human aspects of connecting in person. New develop-
ments such as Foursquare on your phone and the Web site Meetup
.com focus on this—using technology to help people meet face-to-
face rather than just through the technology itself.

Nonetheless, it's hard to argue that technology hasn't drastically
and permanently changed the nature of our friend relationships. Most
likely, at some point in the not-so-distant future, we will connect
with virtually all our friends—rather than just our virtual friends—
through technological intervention. It will just be a question of what
percentage of our interaction is of the flesh-and-blood variety. But it
will always be up to us to make sure that those relationships—in
all their permutations—are as healthy as possible.

4

WHEN YOU CAN NO LONGER BOND OVER BAD CHILI

Making New Friends in the Post-College Era

Much sociological and psychological research has shown that proximity can be extremely conducive to developing and sustaining friendships. And what better definition of *proximity* than to have someone snoring three feet below you every night, or occasionally borrowing your deodorant? (Sorry—you never knew about that last part?) Despite the fact that some of us could produce a horror film based solely on our bad roommate experiences, many positive college relationships are sparked and fueled by seeing one another every day and sharing living and dining quarters. Especially for people who live within their college environs, these types of friendships often take on a family-like quality. It's what I refer to as the Random Tuesday Dinner Phenomenon: nothing breeds closeness and comfort (and occasional contempt!) like having an automatic, default weekday dinner with someone without having to make a date in advance or wonder whether wearing your dark green, admittedly low-cut top will give the wrong impression.

So it's no coincidence that college friendships have the potential to take on a particularly meaningful quality—for many people, they last decades longer than that relatively brief period when you overslept for class together. We often feel that our college friends really "get" us, even if the *us* in question was overusing blue eyeliner during the time that we were closest. As easy as it is while you're in college to long for the end of bad dorm food and think that our real lives will begin only with the "real world," the truth is that friendships—new and old—often take a beating when our confidants are no longer down the hall. And making friends with someone whom you've never seen in sweatpants, or who's never been next to you as you mangled a boy band song in a 3 A.M. spontaneous dorm-room karaoke session, is a different beast entirely.

WHY FRIENDSHIP CAN BE HARDER THAN DATING: STORIES FROM THE TRENCHES

It's often embarrassing for young professionals, when facing their forty-third straight dinner at home with no one but their iPod as company, to begin to acknowledge that they don't have a "group" anymore. Even the notion itself—"I don't have that many friends"—brings back the horrors of slumber party snubs or baskets devoid of pink construction paper Valentines. But quite frequently, this is a predicament in which many young men and women find themselves. It's especially common if you've picked up and started fresh in a new town, or if you've been left alone after a mass exodus of friends (who decided to go off to medical school, back to their hometowns, or to "find themselves" in the Jell-O–wrestling community of Las Vegas). It can make someone feel lonely, embarrassed, and downright unloved to realize that they don't have many potential people to share a comfortable and pleasant meal with. And all too often, it can become a self-perpetuating cycle: the more alone you feel, the more anxiety-provoking it is to try to reach out. How do you go about making friends when there aren't peers in such close proximity to you anymore? How can you kick-start new relationships without coming across as desperate or creepy?

It's a struggle many know well. Says Melinda:

In college, you really take for granted that you can always find someone to eat with, watch TV with, take a walk with, be a study buddy, gossip with, borrow a few bucks from, or give you advice about whatever you're facing. Throughout those years, I couldn't wait to "be on my own"! I longed for that sense of liberation it seemed I was being offered at the end of my degree. However, the harsh reality set in: Congrats! You are on your own and alone! I didn't realize how much I'd be giving up for this new freedom. I moved three hours away to a metropolitan area, and the only person I knew was my best friend's ex-boyfriend. What was I supposed to do? Go to the local Starbucks, scope out the crowd, walk up to someone, and say, "You don't look too crazy—would you like to be my friend? Shall we meet here at the same time tomorrow?"

For many people, this experience also creates a virtual magnifying glass on what they perceive to be their flaws. Says Rebecca:

I definitely have a hard time with being outgoing. Small talk is not my forte. I need someone to be more aggressive in their personality to ensure a connection is made because I'll take a quiet moment as something personal. ("Oh, he/she doesn't like me; let's move on!") I know it's completely ridiculous, but there's still that insecure ten-year-old in my head going, *You are such a dork!* I'm also incredibly sarcastic and sometimes find myself thinking out loud and then questioning, *Crap, was that appropriate?* Because in my mind it was hilarious, but in the real world . . . maybe not.

Many of us have these same concerns. And who among us is blessed with the most perfectly social of personalities? Faux pas and gaffes afflict everyone from time to time. And as we've established, one size does not fit all in relationships. If you were to be equally appealing to everyone—never rubbing anyone the wrong way and never making someone groan—then that would mean you were too bland to be much of a friend. It makes sense that your personality won't—and shouldn't—mesh with absolutely everyone.

But when you're feeling particularly vulnerable and insecure, what you perceive at first as minor quirks in your personality can quickly turn into things you berate and condemn yourself about, convincing you that you're the friend equivalent of a Total Loser.

Complicating things, there's often a wide range of personality facets that we show to people. Perhaps we've got one persona for those who don't yet know us very well and a much different one for those who've seen us before we've blow-dried our hair. It might be even harder to put our true selves out there (wherever "out there" is) if we tend to be more quiet, passive, or flippant among people whom we haven't yet gotten to know. But shyness, for instance, can occasionally come across as coldness or aloofness to others. It's not that you need a personality overhaul. But dealing with some of that nervousness could ensure that you're able to show the "real you" to people a bit sooner.

How else can you work on choosing good friendship matches? Think back to chapter 2 about what you know about yourself. If you don't know what makes you tick (and what brings you to a slow, angry boil), how else will you know what to look for? Think about your personality and the characteristics of the friends that seem to suit you best. Think about what traits you bring to the table, and where people who'd be looking for those qualities would be.

Rebecca, who struggled with meeting people, sums it up:

I think you just have to put yourself out there. You have to have an interest in other people and actively pursue relationships. People are busy, and increasing the size of their network isn't always at the top of their priority list—either as someone attempting to increase their own or as someone who's trying to be "recruited." It does take effort.

HOW TO TAKE THE FIRST STEP, FROM FIRST MEETING TO DEVELOPING A REAL RELATIONSHIP

All too often, a nice connection is made, whether it be at a work function, a party, or a particularly tumultuous time at the Department of Motor Vehicles. *This is someone I could see as a friend,* you think to yourself, becoming suddenly self-conscious as you wonder if this is stalking behavior. (What's the friend equivalent of automatically imagining what your babies would look like the moment that you meet someone?) Even if it's someone you see regularly for other reasons, it often stalls there, despite the desire on both ends.

Lara describes a common conundrum:

I figure people are busy and probably don't have the need/ time/desire for new friends. So I can smile at them when I pick my son up at preschool, and ask how things are, and how was your weekend, and then . . . that's it. We never move past that point, even though I (and possibly they) would like to. It's frustrating.

When the engine's in idle, the notion of following up or going further is so hard. Since you're not going to ask this person for a date (what's the friend equivalent of flirtation?), things quickly become ambiguous. What should the next step be? Friending the person on a social networking Web site or exchanging business cards may be a given, but those have their own pitfalls. With social networking, you might quickly be blended into a sea of hundreds, sharing the same status and priority level as that D-list infomercial actor someone decided to "friend" as a joke.

And business cards can be tough, too. Excited about a particularly cool person you conversed with at a happy hour, you retrieve their card from your wallet a week later. Suddenly, you start to doubt yourself: Did this person really want to connect on a social level, or were they just hoping you'd hook them up with your HR manager (or sell them a decent set of kitchen knives)?

The reality is, you can't know for sure. And here's the kicker: If you're doing something right, you will have screwups, because you'll be taking risks every now and then. So—a reality check: Just as every person you dated did not turn out to be Mr. Right (especially Mr. Felonious Groper!), not every fledgling friendship will turn into the kind that inspires weepy chick flicks, or even trashy sitcoms. In fact, it might turn into something that drives a whole different plot altogether.

From Susanne:

We were both working in a deadline-oriented environment. And living in a big city, I was used to branching out. I asked her if she wanted to see a movie. At first, things were totally pleasant, but after a while it became clear that she was not only ill-suited to our office, but increasingly anxious and neurotic about our friendship. Many times she would stand there at my cubicle, and the tension would rise; she would really get in the way of my getting work done. She would start asking her roommate—a mutual friend—what was going on with me as she started to feel me pull back. The more anxious she got, the more intrusive she was, and the less shot we had at a real friendship. I grew flustered and didn't handle things well. I tried to push her away further, feeding into her anxiety without giving any answers. I wish that I had handled things a little bit differently and more directly.

The fact that not every attempt to become friends will end up in the Hall of Fame doesn't mean you should regret trying, or that you should be embarrassed about the occasional friendship attempt that is a total nonstarter (or a firestarter!). You've got to let go of evaluation concerns a bit; you're still you, still the smart, fun, interesting person you were before, even if someone you thought might be a new friend has now flaked on getting together twice in a row. It's hard to convince yourself that some friendships just won't take, and it's not a judgment on you. Whether it's a missing spark, conflicting schedules, or just the failure to connect in lifestyles or worldviews, it doesn't take anything away from what you offer as a person. View awkward friendship-starting attempts that went nowhere not as a sign of your lack of fabulousness but as necessary, positive steps on the way toward finding someone who fits. *They're progress.* And if you're not having the occasional strikeout, then that means you're not (forgive me!) getting up to bat enough. Just as you shouldn't at all be embarrassed of trying on multiple outfits and thinking, *Eesh! I'd look better in burlap!* before finding the one that really rocks your abs, you also shouldn't be embarrassed of making multiple attempts to connect with different people.

But don't become the equivalent of a relationship tease. Be kind, sensitive, and remember what your frizzy-haired nursery school teacher used to say: Treat others as you want to be treated. Don't try people on without being prepared to put them away properly, no worse for the wear—don't be that person who leaves them in a jumbled, hangerless heap on the floor.

So how does one go about trying on friends? One of the simplest tricks for growing a connection is to pick one aspect of conversation that you've shared in your first meeting (whether online or in person), and continue to follow up with it, asking not-too-intrusive but interested questions.

Check in on the progress of something that was discussed

before, whether it be a job search, an aspect of family drama, a new activity, or even just a foray into the world of making one's own yogurt or cloth napkins. The benefits of this are twofold: it lets the person know you care and were listening, and it also gives the conversation somewhere to go. Remember, nothing keeps a conversation going—real or virtual—like asking a question. And the questions that follow up on something that someone already volunteered are the best kind of all. They personalize your interaction, bringing it from the generic ("Man, it's hot!") to the one-on-one ("Is your AC fixed yet? How are you holding up?"). They build and solidify a bridge between the two of you that a true friendship can grow on.

WHAT NOT TO DO WHEN INITIATING A FRIENDSHIP

All this advice may come off as so simple that you might be rolling your eyes. And yet it can be so hard to follow. If you really think back to the past few stilted conversations that left you wanting to run for the hills, or awkward instant-messaging chats that made you want to enter the Witness Protection Program, you may notice that they all had certain missteps in common. When your friendship is just getting off the ground, here's what *not* to do:

Not ask questions. If you're not giving the other person time to express themselves, then you're simply having a soliloquy without the stage makeup. Nothing is a bigger bore than someone who wants to talk only about themselves without finding ways to connect their experience to the other person's.

Ask bad or inappropriate questions. But sometimes asking the wrong kinds of questions can be worse than the soliloquy. Respect the space and boundaries that should be inherent in any early conversation with another person. That means do not pry about health issues, romantic relationships, political or religious views, financial or career details, or any subject about which the person doesn't want to give much detail.

Miss cues. If the person is trying to change the subject or let the interaction die, by all means, let it happen. Again, listening is every bit as important as talking. Nothing kills the spark of a new connection like someone railroading their way into a topic that the other person is obviously squeamish about or bored with.

Ignore what's been talked about before. If you ask the same questions over and over again, or convey surprise at something that the other person has obviously already mentioned, you're basically screaming, "I'm not really paying attention to you, and I'd probably drive you crazy as a brunch companion!" Occasional lapses of "Oh, yes, you did tell me that. Sorry!" are one thing. But conducting an inquisition full of queries that have already been covered, or repeating for the fourth time some aspect of yourself, is going to send the other person running.

Break confidences. We'll get into this again and again. But unless it's a matter of imminent danger, don't. Just don't.

Let a mistake be a death sentence. So you made a joke you shouldn't have, or you forgot to have your phone on when she was supposed to call you to meet up. Sometimes when a friendship is in the early stages, one false move can feel like a death sentence for the relationship. But it is usually how you handle the mistake that matters far more than the mistake itself. A gracious and concerted apology, and a true attempt to make up for it and not err again, is often more than enough to get the budding friendship right back on track. Instead, people are often paralyzed with self-doubt and let the friendship die a slow, agonizing death out of shame or awkwardness. Don't be so hard on yourself. As long as you didn't do something deliberately hateful, the majority of friendship blunders—even those that happen to friendships in the fledgling stage—can be fixed just by apologizing sincerely and picking up where you left off.

Act like whoever else is in the room is more important than the person you're talking to. If you want to make friends with someone, you need to behave like it. There shouldn't be game-playing or faking hard to get when it comes to platonic relationships (or romance, either, but that's another book!). That means engaging with the person in front of you and making eye contact—not scanning the room or distractedly looking at your watch. Many people have this latter habit, fueled by an overdose of work-networking events, an antsiness to see what's cookin' on their iPhones, or maybe just an obsession with movies about hit men. Three words: *break the habit.* It's getting in the way of your relationships, period. It can make you seem bored, snotty, or totally distractible, even when that's the furthest thing from your intention (or your personality).

Be pushy or anal about plans. For God's sake, if you're trying to start a friendship, don't be the person who has only a three-block radius of where you're willing to eat dinner, or an overbearing worldview about whether to see the late or early movie. If the preview that the other person is getting of you is that you're someone who is as inflexible as a steel wall, then that person is not going to want to stay for your main feature.

Be wishy-washy about plans, or change plans three hundred times. This is arguably as bad as railroading an uninterested party into a kung fu marathon. Maybe you change your mind so many times that the other person can't even remember what you settled on. Or perhaps you say "It's up to you" so often the new friend can't help imagine how excruciating it would be to wait for you to order off a menu for the next ten years. Either way, these tendencies are bad news for beginning friendships. You're basically inviting that person to do a cost/benefit analysis of entering into a friendship with you—and you're putting yourself at a big disadvantage.

Put the burden on the other person in terms of effort, communication, initiation, or money. When you're looking to make a new friend, the process has at least a little something in common with looking to sell a used (or is it *pre-owned?*) vehicle. Basically, you want to make it as easy on the other person as possible. And paying more than their share, transferring subways twice to meet at a spot next to your house, or always having to be the one to start up a text conversation about what's on tap for the weekend is not the way to do so. Once again, in the cost/benefit analysis, your wonderful qualities may appear to come up short. Why not stack the deck in your favor instead?

Be cruel about others. Some people think that any talk about other people is a bad thing. As someone who has discussed Brad and Angelina more than I'd care to admit, I must disagree. I think it's unhelpful to totally ban talking about other people: referencing others is a natural human instinct that serves as a kind of glue for our communal experience. But it's true that certain types of talk can be toxic. When you're talking about others for the purpose of making them look bad, directly or indirectly, or your motives feel cruel, that has no place in the beginning phases of the friendship (or even the later ones, actually). It obviously is bad form, and it victimizes the person being talked about. Plus, it will surely make your new friend wonder what you are going to be saying about them, behind their back, two hours from now.

Try too hard to impress. Just as being cruel about others isn't a great idea, it's also dangerous to succumb to the temptation to extol your own virtues, or the virtues of your relationship with so-and-so. Leave the temptation to name-drop behind. Nothing says *insecure* like your fourth mention of your sister having once dated Vin Diesel's body double. And bear in mind that research generally shows that we tend to like people who are less defensive about their flaws and are able to reveal some vulnerabilities. Treating every platonic date like you are running for office is not appealing.

DEVELOPING A SENSE OF COMMUNITY

Friends offer us many of their psychological benefits, not just from how they make us feel as individuals, but also what the sense of being part of a whole community can bring. Belonging to something—whether it's a church, university, office, or just a particularly rambunctious family (more on that in chapter 9)—brings us a sense of meaning that can be quite powerful. And being part of a group of friends yields this same benefit, as long as the positives of the friendships outweigh the negatives.

Belongingness—the notion that we fit in somewhere in the grand scheme of things—imbues us with comfort and security. And so it's quite important that when we are no longer part of a certain community, we try to seek out that feeling in new ways. When you find yourself without that naturally occurring sense of belonging for the first time, like what typically happens when someone moves to a new city or graduates college, it's important not to forgo it permanently.

Some communities happen almost accidentally. Maybe the people in the apartments on your floor all started watching football together; maybe the people at your dog park started getting together for coffee every Sunday. But you can't count on that.

Here are some ways that you can jump-start the process and possibly strike gold. (Yes, this would technically make you a "community organizer.")

- If you own a pet, search out new dog parks or online message boards about your breed. And if you don't own a pet but want one, get one! Or foster one. Or volunteer with them. Offer your services as a dog walker or pet sitter.
- Eat the cost of an extra ticket to someplace you'd like to go, like a show or a sporting event, and offer it to your entire office or community mailing list. Yes, there's the scary possibility that that dude Frank with the clean-microwave fixation might be the one to take you up on the offer. But here's a trick: Say that the names of everyone who responds to your offer by a certain time will get put in a hat and that

you'll do a drawing. Just don't promise that the drawing will be blind, and do it privately: simply choose whom you want to go with and tell them they won. I'll keep your secret!

- If you're into nature, look into getting a small plot in a community garden. If you have a balcony or any slice of yard where a pot can fit, try to grow some herbs (not that kind!) to give away to neighbors.

- Become known as the person who has a specific social role in the office, whether it's sending around the birthday cards, bringing in cookies after a particularly arduous round of staff meetings, or handling the Super Bowl pools.

- Get involved in volunteer work. Donate time and effort instead of writing checks or entering in your credit card number. From elementary schools to soup kitchens to animal shelters to environmental groups, the possibilities are endless, and you'll meet a ton of like-minded local individuals.

- Start going to the same hairstylist or pedicurist or whatever it is that floats your boat. And remember what she says from time to time. Make small talk that can turn into more. Talk about your interests, and you may be surprised to hear whom else she knows.

- Connect with the local alumni association of your school, if there is one.

- Join an athletic league—you don't have to be the second coming of Serena Williams. There are all kinds of groups for beginner adults. Or start training for a race with a charity team.

- Join a fantasy sports team or fantasy investment team.

- If you're crafty, find a local craft store or yarn shop and look into classes or open sessions there.

- Get on your neighborhood LISTSERV, not just to complain about the house whose lawn hasn't been mowed since the

Clinton administration, but maybe to start a book club, game night, or community cleanup.

- Look into joining a commuter carpool.
- If you have a local coffee shop and have work that you sometimes do at home, do some work there instead. (Note: this is not a great idea if your work is producing or starring in adult films.) Even if it takes you forever to start conversing with some of the people there, you will at least feel part of the neighborhood, which will give you a boost.
- Try to find a local online message board about something that you're interested in. Maybe it's movies, politics, restaurants, or just a meetup for fans of a popular blog. Start commenting more on the sites you do visit, and keep an eye out for people who are local.
- Seek out a church, particularly one that has an active young-adult fellowship.
- Take a class—another language, martial arts, belly dancing, cooking, climbing, Pilates, horticulture, cake decorating, anything. You'll have an added opportunity for becoming part of a community if it's the type of place that you have to return to practice or use the facility (yoga or pottery, for instance).
- If you can't think of any interests you want to pursue, stumble into some. Sites such as Meetup.com specialize in bringing groups of like-minded strangers together. Browse around and get inspired.

LIES WE TELL OURSELVES THAT SABOTAGE OUR FRIENDSHIP QUEST

Of course, even after planting these seeds (which is admittedly harder for the less outgoing among us), it's easy to sabotage ourselves by being afraid to take the next active step in a friendship. Often, as we touched on, this is caused by negative thought patterns that prevent us from taking the risk of developing a connection. Do any of the excuses below sound like you when faced with trying to take a relationship further?

"They have so many friends already!" But real life is not Facebook; no one comes in with a red buzzer once you reach a certain number. And one solid, rich, deep friendship is often worth as much as the fifty that preceded it.

"They're too pretty/funny/smart for me." Again, we can never be completely objective about ourselves. You may very well have qualities that she admires; she could even be having the same insecurities about how she stacks up against you.

"It's not worth it, since she/I will be here for only a little while." News flash: Plans change. You might choose not to get to know your new neighbor because your lease is up in four months. Or you might not let yourself get close to that friend of a friend who seems so interesting and funny because you're certain that you're headed for a cross-country move by next spring. But all too often, we tell ourselves this, and then plans change and we stay put. And we've squandered the opportunity to grow a real friendship. The lack of interest we showed while we were not letting ourselves get involved might have permanently cooled the possibility of that relationship.

"She and I have nothing in common." Again, by now you might have realized that sometimes the most exciting friendships occur where the common ground is not immediate. By definition, if there is something about her that makes you want to be her friend, that is enough commonality to start with!

"I don't have very many interesting things to share." If you really believe this, you need to do a reality check of all that you've brought to other friendships. And if it's a genuine problem, you

can remedy it by expanding your horizons from the activities mentioned earlier.

"I'm too busy." This may be the case. But be honest with yourself about what you're busy with. Are you spending time keeping up "friendships" that will never lose their quotation marks? Are you busy flitting around with relationships that don't really sustain you, and using that as an excuse—perhaps even without realizing it—not to seek out deeper relationships? Or is your busyness itself a problem that legitimately gets in the way of friendships? Much like the workaholic spouse who finds his or her marriage crumbling into oblivion, some people could use a reality check when their job or other activities have become their only companion and confidant. What are you hiding from?

"I don't want to start all over again with a new group." This temptation is understandable. But even the Golden Girls needed to branch out a bit. It's easy for young adults to fall into the trap of feeling like certain aspects of their lives should already be set as fixed entities rather than works in progress. But you might be surprised to know that chances are, some of the people who will make the most difference in your life—romantically, platonically, or family-ly—you haven't even met yet. Just as we can't yet imagine what fashions will be found attractive twelve years from now (though I'm hoping guyliner won't be involved!), neither can we be sure what friends we might meet that could make a true difference, for the better, in our lives. Why seal yourself off in a time capsule?

"She's friends with Angela, and I don't like Angela." This may be true. But would *you* always want to be judged by every aspect of every single one of *your* friends? How horrified would you be if some particularly amazing person who could add so much to your life was avoiding getting to know you because they once had a spat with one of your roommates?

ONCE YOU'RE IN IT: HOW NOT TO GET CAUGHT IN THE INERTIA OF RELATIONSHIPS THAT ARE WRONG FOR YOU

Many times, we develop a circle rather passively. For all the effort that goes into attracting the "right" romantic relationships, we are occasionally all too willing to fall into the friendship equivalent of Mr. Wrong without so much as a single doubt.

This is in part because friendships don't tend to have the official standing in our lives that romantic relationships—especially monogamous ones—do. Since we might have dozens of different friendships, all of them serving different roles in our lives, it can be easier to slip into bad patterns without anyone doing an intervention.

Signs That You're Falling into an Unhealthy Relationship

- You're secretly ashamed of something you've started doing with your friends.
- Your friends themselves are not healthy, and are not making any effort to be.
- You're constantly teased about being more upstanding or wholesome than your friends.
- You find yourself censoring aspects of your friendships, either when you think about them, or when you talk to your other friends or family about them.

You'll learn more about how to walk away from these friendships in chapter 10. But let those warnings simmer a bit because it's easy to fall into the wrong crowd long past the stage of curfews and homecoming dances.

HOW COLLEGE FRIENDSHIPS ARE DIFFERENT FROM LATER FRIENDSHIPS AND WHY THAT'S OKAY

It's important, ultimately, to make sure not to idealize your past friendships, especially when you're in a new dry spell. This risk is especially strong when entering new life phases. For instance, when you're alone in your new cockroach-infested studio apartment, or working in some awful job where your coworkers make your skin crawl, it's easy to fabricate a misleading glow around the halcyon days of college buddyhood. Yes, that person held your hair off your face when you vomited (you will never touch Goldschläger again!), and yes, your rapport seemed so easy as you giggled your way through four years together. But there's a sheen that develops over time, and we need to be careful we don't pretend these relationships were perfect, or that their quality will never again be attainable.

There's also something to be said for the role of increasing self-awareness as you get older. As people leave their teen and adolescent years behind and grow more independent, many friendships initiated as adults are naturally imbued with more autonomy and choice, surpassing the randomness of being thrown together in a dorm room. The trick is making sure you are an active participant in maintaining and nourishing your friendships, no matter how they were formed. You always must continue to check in about who you are and whether or not the relationship is healthy. Regardless of how old you or the friendship is, autopilot can be dangerous.

And never does autopilot apply more than in workplace environments. Read on for a primer on the drama of the friend/coworker hybrid.

5

FRIENDS AND WORK

Like Oil and Water, or Oil and Fire?

Though it's cringeworthy to think about, most working adults spend an inordinately large amount of their waking hours in the workplace. (And for those who have particularly boring staff meetings, they spend plenty of their sleeping hours there, too.) Add to that the occasional workplace "social" events, from happy hours to holiday parties to picnics, which may or may not be mandatory (and may or may not be "social"), and even your nonworking hours are in jeopardy. The icing on the cake is commuting time, which only seems to be getting longer, despite the growing segment of telecommuters. In short, your workplace can be quite the hog of physical and emotional energy.

But it's not just the nuts and bolts of one's job that matter. In actuality, many professionals define "the people" as one of the top reasons they love or loathe their jobs. The relationships between you and your coworkers, clients, underlings, and supervisors are often cited as the biggest causes of bliss or stress—and for some people, they can even outweigh financial considerations. In a particularly bad job (where crying and panic attacks are par for the course in the staff bathroom), a coworker can be the lifeline that helps you through.

But rarely is the role of the coworker—and the hybrid known as the colleague/friend combo—as clear-cut and positive as that. Even for those who adore their coworkers, there are often complications and questions about the nature of your relationship. A good collegial rapport can collapse under the intricacies of a more personal friendship. On the other hand, two people who would easily be friends out of the office may find that as cubemates or boardroom companions, their friendship hits unexpected bumps in the road.

IS THAT SARAN WRAP AROUND YOUR CUBE? (DRAWING APPROPRIATE WORK BOUNDARIES)

There's some indication that for younger incoming generations of workers, this problem is even more prevalent. Says Amy Joyce, former work/life columnist for *The Washington Post* and author of *I Went to College for This?*:

> I think younger workers just starting out are used to a more personal and casual relationship with everyone: peers, bosses, relatives. A lot of this is due to how we use things like Facebook and Twitter. So I believe these workers are creating closer relationships with folks than if they were born a generation ago. We now use phrases like *work spouse* (for that person of the opposite sex whom you are attached to at work all day long and can't make a run to Starbucks without), go out with our work colleagues, and spend time on weekends with workmates. The lines that used to be drawn between coworkers or even workers and bosses have gotten much fuzzier.

Should you be "real" friends with your officemates? Is it unwise to drink at the office party? Must you invite your boss to your wedding? Should you accept your colleague's Facebook friend request? Should you not have made that joke about carnies at the staff meeting?

6 COMMON PiTFALLS OF WORK FRiENDSHiPS

The quandaries of workplace engagement are many, and I won't pretend to answer every single aspect of them here. (Carnival worker humor is complicated, at best.) But we can start by identifying the most common problems that crop up as you dance on the line between professional and friend relationships, and to establish some general principles to see you through the rest.

1. Creating an all-for-one and one-for-all work partnership

If you and your closer-than-close coworker are thought of as a package deal, you're both liable to go down with the ship when one of you makes a mistake. Being bosom buddies with a coworker—where your supervisor two rungs up the ladder is not completely aware that you are even two different people—doesn't help either of you. People have a hard enough time remembering names and faces without you making them think that you and your workmate are interchangeable. The more physical time that you're hanging around a coworker at the office (it's a bad sign if your bladders are in sync because of all the dual bathroom and coffee breaks), the less you'll be seen as an individual with your own strengths and credentials. Even worse, if your coworker slips up—and no matter what kind of friendship you have, you can never truly be sure how good she is with those TPS reports—then you are guilty by association. (The "work husband" concept carries these perils as well.)

2. Letting your friendship get in the way of your productivity, progress, or ambition

This can happen so passively that you might not notice at first. One month, you're in a groove, working through lunch and earning accolades. The next, you're jetting off to a too-long lunch pedicure with your colleague-in-crime, or giggling a little too hard at her off-color joke about nuns, making your boss shoot eye-darts not just at her but at you as well.

Yes, there's room for smiles at the office: an environment devoid of laughter would be draining indeed. But you must make sure that it's you and you alone choosing the parameters of your professional image. If you want to slack off, slack off, but make it a conscious decision. Don't get pulled into it because Jessica from one desk over is doing it, like the time you smoked that cigarette after homeroom.

3. Expecting to be treated as a friend instead of a coworker when the going gets rough

Different offices draw different lines between professional and personal, and it's important to know where yours lies. Maybe your boss sending you a fruit basket and telling you not to worry about the time you missed while out for surgery is par for the course. If so, you're quite lucky! If not, you can't expect it. While being treated with respect and fairness is every worker's right, sometimes people believe they deserve a little extra if they have developed a personal or pseudo-personal relationship with the boss. Don't fall for it. Most likely, your boss will expect you to follow rules and procedures about everything from lunch breaks to time off to office cleanliness, whether you bike in together or not.

4. Drawing inadequate boundaries

It seemed like a good idea at the time to let your cubemate know about your blog, or to reveal to your new intern that you went through a bit of a hallucinogenic phase in high school. But it might not have been so good. In fact, it might have been really, really bad. It's often hard, when you're finding your own style in a new work-group or as a first-time manager, to know where to draw the line between being warm and collegial and being unprofessional. There is no doubt that some amazing and long-term friendships have grown from the workplace. But busting down the professional boundaries too soon or with too many people is bound to jeopardize your professional status. Self-revelation is not the only way in which boundaries can get broken. Oversoliciting for your daughter's Girl Scout cookies, posting a lot of political paraphernalia, and just having particularly loud personal phone calls can all drive a sledgehammer through appropriate work boundaries.

With all these limits, you might be prone to ask, How can I possibly become someone's friend this way? It might seem like I'm asking you to stay buttoned up and bored throughout your entire workday. But that's not it at all. It's about respecting the boundaries enough at the beginning that you build a healthy foundation for a possible relationship later on. Once that's there, you both can nudge the boundary together—reciprocally and comfortably—over a gradual and steady period of growing more personally close. But for one of you to steamroll over the line takes away the potential for a genuine and healthy friendship to develop. Instead, it leaves you extremely vulnerable to being deemed unprofessional, getting fired, sued, or worse.

5. Overindulging in gossip

What would a workplace be without a little dirt? It's hard to imagine; talking about other people is how humans tend to connect and bond. As I've mentioned, I doubt an all-out ban on discussing others is wise (or realistic!). But being known as the office gossip or gaining a reputation for being indiscreet or hurtful can easily get in the way of moving forward, professionally and personally.

6. Getting sucked into having your coworkers be your main social circle

Putting all your eggs in one basket this way can be treacherous. If you work long hours or in a particularly emotional environment, it's easy to start thinking of the people you work with as part of your family. The close quarters, steady companionship, and natural highs and lows of working together can do for friendships what they often do for romances—ignite sparks and cement bonds. (High school theater class, anyone?) But they can also have the decidedly negative impact of forcing you to let go of some of the non-work influences and outside perspectives in your life. And the more you get sucked into a work-only mind-set, the more you need some outside space. You might see yourself spending significantly less time with family, friends, and romantic partners, and branching out less and less, giving up activities that you can no longer squeeze in or that don't seem to fit in with your professional identity. It's fine to be altered by a job, but to be totally enveloped by it is risky. All of a sudden, you have no outside supports to warn you if your job has grown toxic, you're not taking care of yourself, or your stress levels are problematic. Leave some space on your friend list for people who don't see you all day.

As a general rule, it's important to remember that what makes a good coworker is not necessarily what makes a good friend. The match between colleague and buddy may not be made in heaven. In addition, people's personality traits may convey differently at work than they do at home. While the rare person may be one and the same with her friends, dates, coworkers, and parents, someone else may be putting on a dual-personality performance worthy of an Academy Award. Don't expect, while partnering up and growing closer to a coworker, that what you'll see during a weekend get-together will automatically have the same quality that makes your coffee breaks worthwhile. You might just find yourself stammering to find common ground until you start talking about work again!

Here's an all-too-common example of the lines that can get complicated between friend and coworker, from Ben:

I met Kayla at work and we talked all the time, becoming really good buds. She wasn't on my same work team. I convinced her to transfer to a position like mine, and it turned out she was awful at it. She moved to the desk across from me and would scream and throw fits because she couldn't get something. I'd try to support her—sit with her and say it takes time. I would be the one that would have to calm her down. She ended up getting laid off. I felt bad because, to be honest, she probably wouldn't have gotten laid off if she had stayed in her old position.

WHEN CONFLICT APPEARS: HOW NOT TO END UP JOBLESS AND FRIENDLESS

Even if you behave perfectly, work/friendship conflicts can—and will—happen. Here are some common issues:

A *"friend" is using something in your personal life against you at work.* Sometimes relationship drama, financial difficulties, or an illness might be alluded to in conversation with a colleague, only to be brought up later to make you look bad. Though it's too late to take back revealing the sensitive information, you can try to stop its harm by being assertive and discreet. Privately convey to your "friend" that you would appreciate it if she refrained from spreading around your personal business, and if push comes to shove, declare to whoever else is involved that you think the discussion is inappropriate. Be prepared to prove your colleague wrong by trying your best to pull it together and minimize the issue's effects on your work performance. There's a good chance that your coworker might end up looking petty and untrustworthy if their information is irrelevant to your professional image.

A *friend asks or expects you to "hook her up"—with an interview, contract, phone number, or inside info, making you uncomfortable.* Maybe you have no idea what her work credentials are, or you know they're awful and you don't think she'd last at your company for a second. Maybe you worked really hard to cultivate a certain connection or reputation and you resent that she wants to piggyback on it. Remember that being a friend is not synonymous with sacrificing your own image or career. So, be honest (sort of). Tell her you don't think it would go over too well—for her or for you—to try to grease the wheels too much. Offer her some token piece of help that you feel okay with as a peace offering (the name of an easily Googlable contact, for instance), and don't string her along once you've drawn the line.

Your friend asks you to keep a secret that could be harmful to your workplace or your professional reputation. Ideally, this is prevented before you hear it. If she asks if she can tell you something in confidence and you think it might not be wise, be honest and say you'd rather not hear it if it's going to put you in an awkward position.

If you've already accepted the secret, things are trickier. All bets are off if you are being asked to keep confidential something that runs directly afoul of legal or ethical concerns. (You're not a psychologist, after all!) Ultimately, your conscience must be your guide, whether your role is to be whistle-blower or confessional.

Your friend got fired or laid off, and is enraged with your company. You're just grateful to have a job, and don't know how to respond. It's a tricky balance, to be sure, but empathy for your friend's plight need not make you an accomplice to toilet-papering your entire workplace. Keep up contact with him through lunches or phone calls outside of work, but try not to let his venom give you survivor's guilt: you can feel sorry for him as a friend, but you still need a paycheck. Be patient in listening to his woes without letting him force you to berate your company.

Your friend wants to recruit you for some crusade, whether to speak up against a boss or get some office kitchen policy changed, and you just don't feel comfortable with it. Again, gentle honesty is best. "Julie, I want to support you in any way I can, but I just don't feel comfortable signing on to this. I know my unease with it would do more harm than good."

Your coworker is always hitting you up for charity participation, or with religious talk and so on. It can hereby become this book's mantra: gentle but firm. "No, thank you," said with a smile and a graceful change of subject, can go a long way. Over and over, and over again.

You are now a boss and have not developed appropriate boundaries with your underlings. You've got to start somewhere. Though it might be jarring to change personalities entirely from jocular colleague to hard-nosed supervisor, it is totally natural that there will at least be some alteration in the dynamic between you and your previous equals when you take on a position that elevates you. If you'd like, address the issue directly. You might also seek advice from work mentors; this is a common problem that most people climbing the ladder have dealt with. But this also goes back to the idea of establishing healthy workplace boundaries and a comfortable personal/professional divide from the get-go.

Can all difficulties and workplace awkwardness be avoided? Of course not. But isn't listening to you vent about those issues what your real friends—whether they're from work or outside it—are for?

6

TIT FOR TAT

Being a Better Friend So As to Get Better Friends Back

It's easy to assume that the way to get good friends is simply to choose wisely. Of course this is true, but it's not the whole story. Once you choose good people, you have to make sure that they have chosen well in you. As much as it will make this book sound like it should be reshelved in the children's section, I'll say it: There's simply no way to sustain a good, meaningful friendship without doing your part to be a good friend yourself. Having good friendships entails a certain amount of effort and responsibility.

IT'S NOT ABOUT YOUR STASH OF BRIDESMAID GOWNS: 4 SIGNS YOU'RE A GOOD FRIEND

Many people think they're a good friend, just as they think they're a good driver or snowmobiler—they tend to overestimate their own prowess. But just as you needed to do with your personality traits, you've got to take a step back and try to be as objective as possible. It's best to look for some data.

You seem to have real meaning in people's lives. Once again, it's not about how many followers you have on Twitter. It's about whether people are truly letting you into their lives in meaningful ways. Are you among the first to know someone's good news and bad news, beyond what they post to their online minions? Do people want to introduce you to their families? Do people place importance on your life milestones, and are you appreciated for things that you do? Do you feel privy to people's important moments? Or do you tend to feel more like an afterthought?

You get good feedback about your friendships. Is the idea of hearing "I don't know what I'd do without you!" as unrealistic as an army of pigs soaring over the moon? Or do friends regularly let you know that you mean a lot to them and that they get a kick out of you? Of course, many people are not especially prone to sentimentality. Just because you don't get regular greeting cards riddled with water-color sailboats does not mean that you don't have value to people. But you should be getting occasional validation about the meaning of your friendship, even in the way of gentle but affectionate teasing, and about how people are happy to spend time with you.

You attract good people who are good friends. It sounds circular, but the better friend you are, the better people you'll attract—and the better friends you will have. Does your family compliment you on what good people you have surrounding you? Do your co-workers seem to love that friend who sometimes joins you for lunch? Or are your friends making headlines in other ways, like for armed robbery? Try to be objective about the people closest to you. Would other people have reason to be impressed with them? Would you describe them, as objectively as possible, as solid, admirable individuals? If not, it's time to ask yourself why you aren't aiming higher and what you need to adjust about your own behaviors in order to snag the more desirable prizes.

People seem to feel comfortable around you and treating you well. Are people able to let their guard down around you? Do they seem to find it easy to open up to you? If so, this is generally a good sign that you make people feel at ease. Hopefully, though, you don't make them so at ease that they start to take advantage of you or not respect your boundaries and possessions. It's great that a friend feels she can unwind in your living room and be herself. It's less great if she constantly ransacks your fridge and your closet in the process.

AND SiGNS YOU MiGHT NEED SOME HELP DOiNG BETTER

You can use the signs mentioned above as a basic diagnostic tool. If the news doesn't seem good, you need to consider some things you might have been overlooking.

You are frequently disappointed or let down by your friends. At its most basic, this is a mismatch between your expectations and your friends' abilities to deliver on those expectations. Perhaps this means your friends are not capable of being there for you in the way you need. It could also mean that you are not giving them enough of yourself to work with (or are not doing the things for them that you expect them to do for you).

You feel ganged up on in your group. Do you always feel like the odd woman out? Do you sort of have a "circle," but it often feels they could take you or leave you? Sometimes it's easy to get sucked into a group that's downright toxic. The word *clique* often connotes preteens fighting over hair spray, but adults can be offenders as well. When the need to feel part of the group outweighs the benefit of the individual connections within it, it's time to reevaluate.

You find yourself rationalizing the end of friendship after friendship, with "She's just jealous" or "She turned psycho." It's wise to be wary of any man sporting story after story about his various "psycho" exes. *Why doesn't he learn from his mistakes?* you might ask. *How fantastic can he and his judgment possibly be if he's attracting such bad people?* The same is true of platonic relationships. If you have a long history of having friends who turn out to be "bitches," then there's a hiccup in the process of forming those friendships. Either your evaluations of people need some fine-tuning, you're too passive and get sucked into relationships that you know aren't good for you, or you're doing something in these relationships to make otherwise decent people turn on you.

Your friends know way more about you than you know about them—or the other way around. It's worth repeating: Solid relationships enjoy some semblance of balance. Of course, one of you might be more private than the other; maybe one of you is downright shy while the other gives a daily soliloquy about her workday, and that's part of your dynamic. It might feel totally okay, but when things get too off-balance, the level of intimacy is uneven. It's tough for both people to feel equally valued in the relationship when one person holds the power of having so much more insight into the other's life. In these cases, usually a vast difference in communication styles is to blame. Try to adjust accordingly to meet them a little more where they are. Push yourself a bit to open up more, or conversely, ask more questions to see if things can even out a bit.

12 COMMON FRIENDSHIP DILEMMAS AND HOW TO HANDLE THEM

It should be pretty obvious by now that even the healthiest friendships can hit significant bumps in the road. Sometimes the bumps themselves are meaningful because they alert you to a dynamic that needs to be addressed, or they help you grow together. The key to turning a problem into a positive is to be honest about what's going on and be open to at least a little bit of change.

It's also important to keep in mind the possibility of a self-serving bias. Research shows that many of us have a tendency to blame external circumstances when *we* screw up, but blame other people's inner characteristics when *they* screw up. Sometimes just giving someone a break—and making sure that we're not any harder on them than we'd be on ourselves—is all it takes to get through a rough patch. Nonetheless, there are dilemmas that crop up over and over again in even the most solid friendships:

1. You and your friend are both competing for something.

Maybe it's a job, a guy, or a slot in the western division of the mud-wrestling circuit. Whatever way, the shift from what had always been a collaboration toward something that more closely resembles an all-out competition can be hard to take. You shouldn't let a friendship get in the way of pursuing a dream, but if you're going after something that might rub your friend the wrong way, you must be delicate. Do a realistic assessment of what effects this newfound competition might have on the friendship. And be willing to draw honest boundaries—together. Examples of this might be that you don't ask each other for details about the job interview you're both about to have, or you agree to give each other a few days' breathing space after the grad school rejections go out so that you won't have to talk to each other in the heat of the moment. See if you can work out a mutual solution. Nothing fuels envy and competition like insecurity over whether the other person is on the up-and-up or trying to screw you over. Sometimes, when things go unsaid, it is easy to get so caught up in a dynamic of competition that it becomes chronic: do that for too long, and you'll have the dreaded frenemy of chapter 2.

2. You feel like your friend is not prioritizing your relationship the way you are.

Understandably, it hurts and annoys you when she's forgotten to give your pink trench coat back to you for the fourth time or bailed on her promise to help you move. This frustration is born not just out of the material losses and logistical problems that her oversights create, but also because you didn't seem to rank high enough on her list of priorities to keep her from dropping the ball in the first place. It especially stings when you feel you have been so painstakingly conscientious to be a good friend to her.

Sometimes the slights are less obvious, to the point where you might be wondering if you're being too sensitive or taking things too personally—and it's important to keep that possibility in mind. It's a common hurt to creep into even the most solid friendships: the feeling of being pushed aside, or the nagging thought she's just not paying as much attention to you or that she just doesn't seem to include you in her plans as much as she used to. It's time to have the dreaded talk—or at least a written exchange. And no, this is not the place for IMs or texts or Tweets. Go back in your time machine to the Paleolithic '90s and at least send an e-mail because you need the space, and she needs the time to digest it.

Be gentle but firm, and attempt (very hard!) not to be accusatory. This is best accomplished by making it about your feelings more than about her transgressions. (Use "I've been feeling some distance between us lately" rather than "You seem to be avoiding me.") And try not to come on so strong that she feels like in order to get back on track, you'd need to be joined at the hip. You're not looking to be her stalker, but if the friendship is a strong one that is in any way expected to survive, it'll take stepping up and being honest about the discomfort that has developed.

3. You're starting to wonder if you're being used.

Sometimes there is a fine line between being exploited and naturally being expected to help out. Friendships can never be exactly mutually beneficial. (And yes, if you possess a truck or particularly impressive biceps, you will help your friends move more times than they'll help you. No question.) But there should be some rough semblance of balance. Say one of you has a nicer wardrobe and the other one is prone to borrowing it; one of you has a car and the other doesn't; one of you has a job that gives you backstage passes for four, and the other just gets free chimney sweeping—all of these can create a sense of imbalance. But it doesn't automatically have to be unhealthy. If you're on the receiving end of the benefits, try for small but frequent displays of gratitude, no matter how token or inadequate they might seem. (Ironically, one of the most frequent reasons that people fail to adequately thank someone for over-the-top generosity is that it feels inadequate "just" to send a card, make dinner, or deliver a bouquet. How sad to fall into this trap, since doing nothing is obviously the most inadequate thing of all!) Even just a note on your nicest stationery, a homemade meal, or fresh flowers can go a long way toward making someone feel that their kindness is being acknowledged.

If you're the one feeling like you're giving without acknowledgment, first, take a break on being the supplier. The reaction will tell you a lot. Maybe it will dawn on your friend that she hasn't been appreciative enough, and so she'll step up the gratitude. Or she might not seem to notice, in which case you should reevaluate how much she really wanted what you were giving. (Constantly offering people random things that you expect them to accept and be exceedingly grateful for is a bad-friend move in itself.) Still another possible outcome is that she might ask you why the supply of tickets/sweaters/rides/martinis has dried up, and you can try to have an honest talk about how you felt like her enthusiasm had waned. She might get the hint and make things better, or you might decide that you're being used and think about moving on.

4. A mutual friend you don't like is becoming the other woman.

Triangles aren't just for love relationships. In fact, in friendships, the shapes can get downright scary—the platonic pentagon is certainly not uncommon.

Ask yourself why you don't like this person. Does jealousy play a role? Can you imagine, even just the tiniest bit, what your friend sees in her? Give some thought to how you can occupy a different sphere than your nemesis does. As we've discussed, no two friends play exactly the same role in someone's life, and there's no cap on the number of friends you can have. Continue to be yourself, of course—no need to become her hockey partner if you've never stepped on the ice. But don't be afraid of branching out in a different direction. So she's got a new workout buddy; you might still have movie night. So she seems to have chosen someone else to vent about her boss to; you can still make her laugh harder than anyone.

It also can be helpful to be honest about feeling eclipsed, which is best done with gentle humor. "Hey, I notice you've been spending a lot of time with Jessica. Honestly, I don't seem to get her like I get you. So she better not take my place in our stitch-and-bitch sessions!"

5. Your friend is taking you down an unhealthy path.

Research shows that peer groups are extremely strong influences on our lifestyles and individual behaviors, for better or for worse—and that effect doesn't end when we stop using pimple cream. Studies have found that even well into adulthood, who your friends are helps predict everything from your weight to your happiness to the amount of sleep you get. But it's often hard to objectively assess the effects of our own friends.

This is true for a variety of reasons: First, we have a vested interest in the outcome. If we like our friends, we presumably want to continue hanging out with them, so we're not going to be so quick to see their jerk/dominatrix/drug-pusher/saboteur qualities. Plus, when we care about people, we like to see the good in them, and so our affection for them might blind us to some of their unsavory traits, just as in romantic relationships. Additionally, the better we know someone, the more ammunition we have to try to explain away our negative gut feelings. That is to say, the more connected we are to someone, the more we can make excuses for them.

Also, as friendships grow and we pick up behaviors by associating with these friends, the changes can be very gradual. We might not see it coming: One day we're having an extra margarita because our friends are giggling and the drinks look so fresh and fruity; a year or two later, we're bringing a flask over to *Desperate Housewives* night.

This is where people outside your immediate closest friend circle— family members, old friends who have moved away but you're still in touch with, trusted coworkers, and new friends—can be helpful. They might have picked up on something but not wanted to rain on your parade, or they might have been afraid to confront you about it, an even worse sign. But bringing up your concerns, and getting their feedback in a way that makes it okay for them to be honest, can give you another layer of insight. If you are capable of being somewhat objective, you can also try to write down "data" on your friends, listing their qualities as drily as possible so that you can reevaluate, from a distance, whether they sound like people you should be entangling with—or running from.

You are more likely to get into these situations if you often play the role of trying to "save" your friends. Maybe you're the type who's drawn to people who need help; that's no crime. And if they truly need help, it's not that you must dump them, and it doesn't make them bad people if they have unhealthy habits. But you really must protect yourself from sliding down with them. (Paramedics know this rule well: Don't let yourself become one of the injured. That doesn't help anyone in the least.)

6. You've been betrayed by your friend, and you don't know whether you can let go of your anger.

Don't detonate your friendship without giving yourself a cooling-off period. After you have gotten out of crisis-response mode, you'll need to attempt to be objective about how your friend has tried to make right the offense. Can she change? Is there a real reason why it won't happen again? Do you feel like she has come clean, or is there still confusion and suspicion? Do you still feel like you know her? Be honest when figuring out whether your friendship is worth going back to.

7. You have several distinct patches of friendships but don't feel like you have a "group." You dread the idea of all your friends being together because you doubt they'd get along.

Many people have this issue, especially as they pick up in a new place and develop various circles through various avenues. If you do want to try to unite these groups somewhat, take the pressure off and start small. Having all your friends together on some blowout spa weekend might be overwhelming for all of them. (It often happens with bachelorette parties, though—see chapter 7.) Instead, pick two people who seem to have the most chance of getting along, and invite them to an outing that they're both likely to enjoy.

If you have totally compartmentalized groups of friends, you might attempt to evaluate whether something about your personality is being compartmentalized as well. Sometimes, when we're afraid to show our true selves, we take to putting on masks that are a better match to the situation we're in than to who *we* really are.

8. You feel that you're growing apart.

This is a chapter in itself! See chapter 7 and chapter 10 if the verdict doesn't look good.

9. More money, more problems!

If it didn't make me sound like such a fossil, I would bring up the *Friends* episode where the "poorer" members of the sextet (since when is wearing designer clothes in a huge Manhattan apartment poor?) confront the more affluent over the strain of money differences. Money issues can often cause turmoil in relationships, and they can be saturated in awkwardness. Maybe your friend has long owed you money. Maybe she's expecting you to spend more on her wedding than you budgeted for. Or perhaps she never agrees to the cheaper happy hour, or always expects you to split the check evenly when she orders far more extravagantly. Gentle honesty is the best way to ensure that resentment doesn't build over time. Try to work out a compromise that's within both of your comfort zones. Maybe this means going out to dinner but only ordering dessert. (Don't do this too often, or others might start feeling uncomfortable enough to buy your meal.) But be willing to accept that if someone's circumstances are vastly different from yours, there might just be things you'll have to miss (whether because you're going out without them, or you're not going at all).

10. Your friend is romantically involved with someone you don't like, or someone you think is bad for her.

Here it's important to recognize the limits and boundaries of your role, and to really examine why it is you don't like the person. Could it be that you're jealous—either of your friend who now seems so happy, or your friend's new romantic partner, who now seems to be taking over the role of her confidant?

Certainly, if there is reason to suspect mistreatment, whether physical or emotional, you need to confront your friend. But otherwise, you do have to keep in mind the boundaries of your position in your friend's life. You may have to step back gently, knowing that you might have to toast them someday—so don't say anything you'll regret. At the same time, it's a good idea to discreetly solicit feedback from other friends to see if they share some of the same concerns. Remember, though, that there's a fine line between doing so and just whaling on someone behind their back. While you need not lie to your friend and give their new love a ringing endorsement, you must be gentle in bringing up something about them that bothers you.

11. Your friend is going through something very difficult, and you're starting to feel the strain and confusion of not knowing how to help her.

It is *never* a copout to suggest to a friend that she could use an extra hand. In fact, it's pretty much the best thing you can do for someone who is seriously struggling. Many people are afraid to bring up the idea of therapy, but it's often the only suggestion that makes sense. See more in chapter 11 for how to navigate this conversation.

12. Your friend is doing something that you disapprove of.

Maybe you've been trying so hard not to judge, but you just can't stomach her new habit. It's a conundrum that can tear a friendship apart—and it's often combined with the dilemma of not liking a friend's romantic partner. Anya explains how she stuck to her beliefs and the ramifications that followed:

> My friend tried to force me to be friends with her married boss, whom she was having an affair with. She wanted me and my boyfriend to go on double dates with them; she would bring him over and say, "You should talk to him! He's a really great guy!" Then she'd sit me down later and say, "You need to make an effort; he's really important to me." And I'd think, *No, he goes home to his wife!* It was completely against all my beliefs. There are things you can overlook—like disagree-

ments about politics, or different religions. But when someone tries to force something against your beliefs down your throat, you might have to part ways because you just can't take it anymore.

Sure enough, that friendship eventually ended; seeing eye to eye just got too difficult. In general, when discussing a difference in values with your friend, you should always try to frame the discussion as being about wanting what's best for them, or else you risk coming across as sanctimonious. Depending on how integral this issue is to her life, it might be something you can overlook. Having to swallow your morals every time you talk, however, will probably make you want to pull the plug eventually.

YOU DID *WHAT?* CLASSIC FRIENDSHIP BLUNDERS YOU SHOULD *NEVER* MAKE

- *Trying too hard to bring business into a friendship*

    With the economy about as robust as the biceps at a bingo hall, it seems that more and more people are jockeying to get you to buy their lotions, jewelry, or cooking utensils. Or maybe they're gunning for you to sell those products for them while they sit on top of the pyramid drinking martinis in their private plane (um . . . yeah, right). The problem is, many of these people are your friends, or at the very least, your "friends."

    Yes, it's natural when you become a sales associate for a new brand of foot exfoliation (it's amazing!) to look to your friends as the first line of revenue. Many marketing schemes (whether they're pyramids, octagons, or those squiggly, vertigo-inducing dodecahedrons) explicitly encourage this. But before you start hitting everyone up, you've got to ask yourself, What am I really doing here? Not just, *Why am I selling a skin cream made from jojoba beads?* but *Why am I risking making the people whom I'm closest to severely uncomfortable?*

This isn't to say that you can't let them know what you're doing and invite them to become your customer (or co-seller, or whatever). But nix the high pressure and give them a chance to back away. Don't hound them. Don't repeat your pitch to the point where they're ducking to avoid you in the produce aisle. And don't, under any circumstances, be anything less than clear about your holiday party being a place where you'll be selling your merchandise.

• *Treating your friendship as if it has an ON/OFF/STANDBY switch*

We've all heard of them—the women whose dating patterns you can track by whether or not they're returning your calls. Once they get involved with someone, they disappear. Yes, we're all rolling our eyes. But it's not enough for me simply to entreat of all of you, "Don't be *that* girl!" Because if you are indeed that girl, you might not even realize it.

Everyone can benefit from examining their patterns. Maybe every time you're involved with a new job, a new project, a new pet, or a new affair with a Coach purse you notice that you distance yourself from your friends. Perhaps they've even joked about this and you haven't taken them seriously, or you wrote them off as being jealous. Maybe you stubbornly declared that it's only natural that when things in your life get busy (or *you* get busy!), you don't have as much time for them. But if it's a major change—say, from a standing Friday Netflix night to not seeing them for weeks at a time—think about what that means for the dynamic of your friendship. How is it fair that you are the only one controlling its pace and intensity? What does it say about the relationship that it's only your own preferences that are running the show? How can they rely on you when you're so inconsistent, or you make yourself so scarce? Don't just assume they'll be there on standby to pick up the pieces (or don the aqua satin dress at the wedding).

You might be newly in love and wanting to spend every second with your significant other. You might be caught up with a project at work that makes you feel like not returning their calls. It might not feel as fun to be with your friends right now, especially if they happen to be going through stuff that puts them at odds with your happiness (or stress). But deep, true friendships require at least a modicum of continuity. Your friends might indeed understand that you pull back every once in a while—as they should—but pulling back and pulling a disappearing act are different things entirely. If it's been a while, return that phone call, even if you're exhausted after your newly long workdays. Sacrifice an occasional night of new relationship hot-lovin' for a girls' night in. It won't kill you, but *not* doing so can begin the slow death of your friendship.

If you are on the other side, the one who's pushed to the back burner every time there's a new job or new Jason, consider talking to your friend about the pattern. And be willing to do it gently and sensitively enough that you don't run the risk of making them feel defensive. It might be complicated in that maybe you *are* jealous in some way. Maybe you're single and wish you had Saturday-night plans that you actually needed lipstick for, or maybe you're involved with someone but don't have the type of passion that makes you want to run into that person's arms every free second. Separate this slight envy (it's okay—you can admit it!) from the major beef of your argument. If you're speaking mainly out of jealousy, you'll only give them more ammunition.

Sample script: "I wish I saw more of you lately. I'm really excited about you and Mike, but please don't let him take my place!" or "I know you're really stressed at work, but I hope it doesn't make you too exhausted to hang out every once in a while. Maybe a pedicure can rejuvenate your spirits?"

- *Revealing something that was said in confidence, unless it's a matter of absolute and imminent danger—or trying to jockey up the friendship totem pole by cutting others down*

Betraying a secret or revealing something said in confidence goes against both the person whose trust you are breaking and the person to whom you are blabbing. Maybe it's because I'm a psychologist and am used to sitting on sensitive (and let's be honest: juicy!) information indefinitely, but I must take a hard line on this. People occasionally attempt to grow a friendship with Person A by revealing a dirty secret about Person B. And there are few worse ways to begin a relationship. So, cut it out. Of course it can be hurtful if you feel eclipsed by Person B. And so the urge to state your case—overtly or covertly—about why you should be head honcho over them is understandable. But it can all too easily segue into a stealth campaign of undercutting other friends in the group, whether passively, aggressively, or passive-aggressively. Resist the urge. Think about what you're doing: How is it in your friend's best interest to make her other friends look bad? Why is limiting her social support something you would aim to

do to someone you care about? And why are you so insecure in your own value to her that you think it's necessary
to bring others down? It doesn't say a lot about what you
believe you can offer.

- *Convincing yourself you don't "need" certain friends anymore,
  solely because of a change of status, children, marriage, job, or
  location*

Certainly, as life transitions happen, your daily entou-
rage may evolve. Rare is the father or mother who hangs out
solely with childless people after beginning diaper duty. It's
natural, when done in a sensitive and healthy way. But the
extreme version, where you decide to purge whole groups of
friends just because one facet of your life has changed, goes
against the very nature of what real friendship is about. It's
like throwing out a perfectly well-prepared, delicious meal
because you don't like the color of the bowl.

There is an exception to this. If you are trying to make
a significant change for your mental or physical health,
whether by getting sober, cutting out illegal or destructive
behavior, or getting out of an abusive situation, you may
need to make these kinds of abrupt changes. Be gentle but
very firm. You don't have to storm out of their lives in a
huff with a total condemnation of their lifestyles, but when
you need to get away for the good of your health, you deserve to make it a clean break.

- *Forgetting about the need for reciprocity*

If you are always accepting invitations to a friend's
place and never think to invite them someplace yourself,
that will get old to them really quickly. If you are always
the one initiating plans to the point of monopolizing someone's time or overwhelming them with your requests, take
a step back.

- *Trying to take "custody" of friends after a breakup, platonic or romantic*

    If you've been in a long-term romantic relationship that split up, especially if it ended badly, you might be tempted to get possessive and start trying to take ownership of your mutual friends.

    Similarly, if you had an explosive friendship breakup with someone in your circle, you might want to pass out loyalty oaths to your remaining friends. Take a deep breath and don't succumb. Relationships aren't improved by force or pressure. The best you can do for your friends and yourself is to be the type of person whom they'll want to remain friends with. Often that involves being willing to let go a bit, and realizing you don't have to be someone's one-and-only in order to matter immensely. Respect them enough to let them keep relationships with both of you warring parties, if they so desire. It should be their choice to make, not yours.

5 WAYS TO MAKE GOOD FRIENDSHIPS GREATER

It's important to remember that successfully navigating road-blocks is not the only way to strengthen friendships. Sometimes, even your good friendships could use an extra boost:

1. Embrace the little things.

Taking six minutes to pick up your friend's favorite candy when she's feeling low, writing her a note on cool stationery "just because," and remembering to ask about how her dad is doing after his retirement are all simple things that bring a spark to someone's day, and to your own as well.

2. Have a friendship annual exam.

Every so often, think about them, your communication skills with them, whether the balance of reciprocity seems on target, and whether there's something you could be doing more to support them. It's amazing what just a little extra thought toward someone can do to strengthen your bond.

3. Open yourself up to new interests together.

A long-term, "decent enough" friendship can sometimes take on the nature of an in-a-rut marriage, where both participants could desperately use some adrenaline. Starting a new hobby together— even if it's just to make fun of it—can bring a nice new spark.

4. Get healthier together.

Making the commitment to eat better or take walks together or start up yoga can have benefits both physical and emotional. And being in the same boat as you endure the highs and lows of the endeavor can help solidify your commitment toward each other and make you more likely to reach your goals.

5. Take feedback.

Try not to write off your friend's honest complaints—or raves— about you because they're uncomfortable to listen to. Know that the more you're able to consider her thoughts and feelings, the better friend you can be to her.

Knowing how to deal with friendship challenges—and how to improve the relationships that have been sitting awhile—can be just what is needed to breathe new life into your connections. But what happens when instead of new life, there are new circumstances that threaten to tear you apart? Read on.

7

WHEN LIFE CHANGES

How to Keep Friendships Going Without Having
to Buy Stock in an Airline, Watch People Make Out,
or Dine Only at Restaurants with
Animatronic Gorillas

One of the most self-sabotaging perspectives about friendships that young adults can have is that they should somehow have their circle permanently etched into place by the ripe old age of twenty-five or thirty. Similarly, there's often a belief that once you do have good friendships, nothing should ever change within them. But lifestyles are growing ever more transient, economic turmoil is shifting people's employment prospects at a fever pitch, and the sheer volume of information and activities brought on by the Internet has led to unheard-of opportunities for personal growth (on the good side) and personal rot (on the bad). Change happens more quickly—and loudly—than ever before. You simply can't expect that your "gang" today will be your gang five or even two years from now, nor should you. Individual friendships may wax and wane over time, and they can provide unexpected pleasures in their metamorphoses.

The shifts aren't always comfortable, though. Many times they can be agonizing; it's not just a matter of enduring the change, but of doubting whether the friendship will survive at all. And it's easy to wonder if the friendship's survival is worth the effort. Breaking up—or not—with a romantic partner is riddled with all kinds of turmoil. But at least with romances, there's a general understanding of what it means to be in a relationship and what it means to end it. Most monogamous people have fairly clear-cut ideas of whether they're "with" each other or not (past the confusing years of middle school dances, of course).

But for friend relationships, there's no monogamy, rule book, or even breakup process. One person may consider the friendship long gone, whereas another thinks that it's going full speed ahead. One might think you're both moving into exciting new phases of your lives that will be shared with each other, while the other might be doubting that you ever had anything in common in the first place. One of the most common dilemmas while at a friendship crossroads is this: Are we just growing up, or growing apart?

The physical space that comes from logistical changes—graduating or moving across the country, away from your office, or into a different apartment—does not always have to coincide with an increase in psychological space. But often it does. Here are some signs that the friendship, while enduring some changes in its appearance, is still holding on rather healthily:

When you do get time together, you're genuinely curious and interested in catching up. And while you might not understand all the terminology about her job/baby/travels, you actively want to see her happy.

When you are together, you still seem to relate to each other in the same way. While the actual content of your conversation might have changed now that certain external aspects of your lives have diverged, your life philosophies, senses of humor, and conversational styles still mesh well.

The fact that you don't have enough time to catch up with her feels uncomfortable to you. You really do want to return her e-mail or phone call, even if it's gotten put on the back burner. And you're not acting out of guilt or trying to keep up appearances, but out of something that at least approximates the feeling of missing her. Maybe it's been too long and you wish you could just drop her a line or two instead of going through the formalities of catching up. This is a sign that you really do want the connection to continue, but you're getting sucked into a cycle that can kill even the strongest of friendships— the guilt that comes from having waited too long to "adequately" respond to whatever message was sent last. Try to do whatever it takes to plow through and complete the next communiqué, whether it means apologizing for the lateness or brevity (or both). The awkwardness of "I haven't heard from her; she never responded to my list of Boston jokes" can easily harden into ice over time.

Perfectionists are particularly prone to this problem. They miss sending a birthday card, slip up in responding to an Evite, or let too much time pass before getting back to someone about something. All of a sudden, they think, *I've blown it; all is lost.* That's invalid all-or-none thinking. In reality, six months from now, no one would remember the slight, if only the person could just jump back in and make things right.

Another fallacy that plagues friendships and contributes to the strain that develops as people grow and change is the mistaken notion that you have to have a lot in common with your friends— not just in interests, but also in age. Even when people can accept that opposites may attract, they may still believe that they need to be in the same general life stages in order to understand each other. Young women, for example, often want to hang out with other young women, with the belief that that will be who "gets" them best. In truth, there is a certain beauty that comes with friendships that bridge a divide of years, or even decades. Sometimes—as we'll learn later in this chapter—there's a specific friendship chemistry that comes from spanning the ages, connecting with someone who's been in your shoes before.

WEDDiNGS, MARRiAGES, AND BABiES: OH, MY!
DEALiNG WiTH THE EFFECTS OF LiFE TRANSiTiONS
ON FRiENDSHiPS

There is perhaps no greater threat to relationship equilibrium than one person going through a major life change while the other person stands still or takes a different path. Marriage, children, divorce, going back to school, a job promotion, getting one's own place, and other "growing up" alterations can throw a serious kink into the comfortable status quo that has gelled between two people in the friendship. Suddenly, someone is experiencing entirely new circumstances that take up their daily thoughts and attention, not to mention enduring the stress and attitude shifts that such transformations can bring. Your friend might seem worlds away from the person she used to be.

Some friendships will not survive those changes, and it's nothing to be embarrassed about. It shouldn't take away from the positive growth that this person brought to your life. Arguably, you are who you are, at this very moment—even if that involves eating cottage cheese right out of the container, in a Lynyrd Skynyrd T-shirt and no pants—because of your friends. It's helpful to be grateful for what they brought to your life as you mourn their departure.

Other friendships, when faced with a life transition, will remain intact, with some added distance. Still others might grow stronger. And a rarer few will achieve the feat that most people don't think is a possibility—they'll wane but come back later in life richer than ever before. What decides which course a friendship will take? And how can you maximize your chances that the outcome will be good?

Let's take getting engaged and—if that contract with the priest holds tight—getting married. Not only is it one of the biggest and most common life events to happen to women in their twenties and thirties, but it can also have one of the most significant effects on a woman's circle of friends. Wedding planning itself is often the first test of some friendships. The generally assumed notion that the bride is to pick a coterie of thrilled-for-her women to wear matchy-matchy gowns and submit to all sorts of other indignities (though perhaps they'll get pedicures and a gift card out of it!) can drive a wedge into some of the strongest relationships.

Many times, the first problem—even before the bride asks you to wear *that*—is the selection of bridesmaids themselves. We don't generally live our lives quantifying where a line should be drawn between those-who-shall-wear-satin-for-us and those-who-shan't. So naturally, it can be rife with difficulties.

One defense is not to put so much stock in it. There are no wedding police who will invalidate your vows if you choose only your sister as a bridesmaid, or if you have just your parents stand up with you. Nor should you always assume that everyone will be hurt if they're not chosen. Some women, after buying their ninth strapless dress (and no, they won't wear it again), are admittedly relieved to be spared the expense and duties of being your attendant.

Wedding Quandaries Pop Up in Many Other Ways

- She made me a bridesmaid. Must I make her mine?
- The bride is asking *way* too much of me and doesn't understand my financial/time limitations.
- The bride seems to have forgotten that I have a life, too, and hasn't asked about my job/pet/school/boyfriend/family in forever. It's like her wedding is the only thing that matters to her.

(continued)

- I am getting married, and I just don't feel that my bridesmaids are pulling their weight.
- I don't want to include so-and-so in my bridal party because we haven't talked that much in a while/my wedding is really small/I have nineteen sisters. How can I let her know she's still important to me when she's not going to be up at the altar?
- I have a group of friends, but it feels like if I have one of them in my bridal party, I have to have them all. But I don't want to have such a huge bridal party.
- I love my friend, but do not like her fiancé at all. I don't know how comfortable I am with being in her bridal party when I do not have good feelings about this marriage.

For all these questions, it's important to remember what comes first: your friendship, and then way below it, the pomp and circumstance. Ideally, you want your relationships to last much longer than your wedding day, and to endure whether in sweatpants or silk. Go heavy on communication and tokens of appreciation that tell your friends how much they mean to you, and don't take the symbolism of who's "chosen" and who's not too seriously.

And if you're feeling slighted by someone else's choices, follow the same sentiment. Wedding planning involves politicking, and it could be that the bride wasn't able to choose everyone she wanted because she was limiting herself to the same number of attendants her fiancé had, or was steamrolled into including his three sisters or her long-lost cousins. If there's a friendship worth holding on to, you should be able to find it within yourself to get over the fact that for a few hours, you won't be formally recognized with a professional makeup job.

WHEN IS JEALOUSY NORMAL?

With any life transition, sometimes part of the wedge that develops between relevant parties involves the green-eyed monster. Jealousy can wreak havoc on any friendship, but it is most commonly a struggle when someone gets something that the other person wants or wanted to have all to themselves.

It's appropriate to have pangs of *Wow—would've been nice if it were me!* or *Man, why do things come so easy for her?* when your friend scores that perfect triumph. As long as the pangs are rather fleeting and you eventually settle into a comfortable feeling of wanting her to be happy, they're nothing to be concerned about.

Other times, the dynamic of jealousy starts to settle in more permanently. In these cases, it's time to ask yourself whether there's something going on in your life making you resentful and if you might need to get some help with it. Does this happen with more than just a couple of your friends? Or do you have one particular friend who seems to flaunt everything in an increasingly obnoxious way? Or might the growing jealousy be symbolic of the friendship going south for other reasons?

When someone is prone to excessive possessiveness or jealousy, these feelings can change the entire nature of the friendship, as Brooke found out the hard way during her engagement:

We were friends for nine years. The moment I got engaged, she was almost more excited than I was. And then she proceeded to try to run things. Looking back, I see it—how controlling she was, how if she wasn't happy, you couldn't be happy. Her mood dictated the mood of the entire relationship. I've got a strong personality, so I can't understand why I put up with it for as long as I did. She tried to tell me I couldn't have certain bridesmaids, certain colors. But when I eventually planned to move out of our place and in with my fiancé, she flipped out. She was jealous—actually of my fiancé, for taking me away. She tried to guilt-trip me: "How can you leave me? How can you back out of our arrangement to live together?" When I did move out, she went nuts, didn't take my name off any of the joint bills as planned, and then didn't pay the bills. So I got collection notices.

Honestly, there were signs. We had had a falling-out in high school where we didn't talk for a year because of these same behavior patterns—the possessiveness, not being reliable. When I confronted her about it this time, she apologized and said, "I want this to be good. I really want to be your maid of honor." But she eventually stopped responding! Her dress was shipped to me. So I shipped it to her, but I had no idea whether she was going to come to the wedding. The other bridesmaids tried to include her in planning the shower, but she disappeared. It was really odd. How does someone just decide that they don't want to be a part of your life anymore? Even stranger, she cut off all the mutual friends, too.

Rationally speaking, I pretty much counted her out of the wedding, but the emotional part of me was hoping that she would be there. I was nervous: *Do I confront her if she shows up? Do I ignore her? Or do I say, "I'm so glad you're here," and give her a hug?*

She, of course, didn't show up. For two years, it was like a hole that didn't close. I didn't know what happened or why. There's a part of me that still wants her in my life, wants to know if she's okay. And I was worried about her. Did she need help? I spent hours just thinking about it. But how do you fix a situation like that?

I think if she contacted me now, I'd talk to her. It's been six years, and time mellows things. I'd want to see how she's doing. If I spied her somewhere, my heart would probably hit the floor, and I'd think, *What do I do? What do I say?* like seeing an old crush. I don't think I would let her back as a regular part of my life because if somebody's willing to miss your wedding day, then how much can you count on them? Patterns do repeat themselves.

I am usually a trusting person. I take what people say at face value. I believe in the inherent good of people. In a lot of ways, that's a good characteristic to have. But in situations like this, it can come back to bite you in the ass. What did I do wrong?

Common Post-Wedding Quandaries

Of course, after the birdseed and rose petals have been cleaned up, the dilemmas don't end automatically. It's not just wedding planning that can put stress in relationships, it's the whole actually-being-married (just a small detail!) part:

- My friend doesn't invite me out to any girls' nights anymore. It's like she assumes now that I'm married, I can't ever do anything on my own. She just doesn't seem as interested in my life anymore.
- My friend talks about her husband ALL. THE. TIME. They lived together for two years before they got married, so I don't understand why anything has changed. But I can't take it anymore!
- My friend never includes my husband in anything or even asks how he's doing.
- My friend expects me to be just as spontaneous as I was before I got married and seems resentful and annoyed that I need more notice now.
- Now that my friend is married, she couldn't care less about listening to me about what's going on in my dating life, or even my life in general!

(continued)

- I find myself second-guessing everything I say, so as not to end up sounding like a "smug married." (Damn that Bridget Jones!) I feel like I can't talk about what I'm doing in any aspect of my life because I run the risk of being obsessed with being married.
- My friend made some new married friends that she and her husband both hang out with and seems to be ignoring all her single ones. I feel ditched after all I've done for her!
- My friend seems to have grown irritable around me ever since I've been married—is she jealous?

Again, the solution is gentle honesty and one-on-one communication. And try to be more realistic about what you're hoping for. If your friend seems to assume you're a married fuddy-duddy and never calls you for a night out anymore, you might need to make it clearer that she won't offend you if she invites you sans husband. Or if your friend is the one who really has turned into a married fuddy-duddy, you might hint that you miss some of your alone time and that you're willing to make accommodations (like scheduling a week in advance) to get some of that back.

But it's also important to keep perspective. Some friendships might shift as a result of the Great Marriage Divide, and that might even involve them drawing to a close after you've made an honest effort. Sometimes it's the natural course. (Was your mother still in touch with all her bridesmaids by the time you hit elementary school?)

Baby Dilemmas

If diamonds and overpriced serving pieces can pose threats to friendships, imagine the havoc wreaked by diapers and late-night screaming. Here are some common issues that can develop when children—or the journey to acquire them—come into the picture:

- I know my friend has been trying to get pregnant for the longest time. She even suffered a loss. I just found out I am pregnant—it happened quickly—and I want to be sensitive to her feelings but not keep her out of the loop.
- My friend is trying to get pregnant/is pregnant/just had a baby, and it is ALL. SHE. CAN. TALK. ABOUT. I'm not in this boat yet (or maybe I am but would rather discuss other things), and it is driving me nuts.
- Now that my friend is a mom, she expects me to become a huge part of her kids' lives, and I'm not sure I want that. I'm a good brunch partner, not a babysitter.
- I am trying to get pregnant/am pregnant/am the parent of a newborn, and my friend just doesn't seem to *get* it. She expects me to be able to go out just like I used to, or to keep up with everything besides my baby/pregnancy. And she never seems to ask me how I'm doing.
- Now that I am a parent, I can't help feel differently about my nonparent friends. It sounds awful, but their superficial dating problems aren't interesting to me anymore. They feel shallow.

Several general guidelines can help with all these concerns:

Focus on common ground. Yes, you might have to hear stories that you don't relate to or no longer have interest in. But you might still have the same taste in chick flicks, or politics, or New Jersey jokes, or bowling. Try to maximize the connection.

Err on the side of support. You might be frustrated and bored by her seventh discussion of her baby's fever (or that bad blind date). But she probably feels like she's not being heard, and it's weighing on her mind. Give her the attention she seems to need, even if you can spare only a few moments.

Give it more time. Don't even think of ending the friendship in the immediate period after the transition. For one thing, it will feel like abandonment—she needs you now more than ever—and for another, you can't yet adequately predict whether or not you'll be able to find a comfortable new dynamic.

Ask questions. So you don't have any idea what the heck she's talking about when she mentions she's worried about croup? Just ask. So she's discussing some new guy, and you're too sleep-deprived to figure out who he is. (Is this a different Steve from the one from work?) Get the details, and try to catch up.

Sometimes, a life transition doesn't change the people involved as much as it alters how a personality trait manifests itself. Occasionally what we once loved about a friend can turn into what we most hate. In fact, what might even have lent itself to your friendship chemistry—their sarcasm, their indulgence, their drama queen tendencies—can eventually stop serving us so well. Life transitions such as parenthood often crystallize this in an excruciating way, as Latisha saw happen with one of her dearest friends.

Being sort of a know-it-all was always part of her personality, and that was her appeal. She speaks her mind, is very opinionated, and knows what she is all about. She had her first child two years before I did. We were very close through all of that, and then when my son was a newborn, she was invaluable to me, though I realize in retrospect that it was a lot of lecturing I was getting. When I emerged from the fog of the newborn phase and began to get my legs as a parent, it became clear: She was unmistakably a "Sanctimommy." She knew everything. I couldn't have a conversation with her about anything without it turning into a lecture, from nutrition to discipline to car seats. And it just became insufferable. Everything felt like a put-down. One awful moment when I was at her house, I was trying to change my son's diaper, and she literally scooped him away from me and said to him, "Your mommy doesn't know how to change a wiggly boy's diaper."

I started pulling away. What could I have done differently? I should have, in the moment, talked about the way that it made me feel, and I really never did. The few times I did try to say something, it fell on deaf ears. I honestly don't think she knows my feelings. She probably thinks we just grew apart. But how do you tell someone something like that? I think it's who she is, and I'm no longer comfortable with that. It's been awkward to have been so close for so many years and now to be like this. She still contacts me—but I don't want her as my professor.

I do suspect that she's deeply insecure and that this is her way of navigating the world. But there are many wonderful qualities about her that I miss. I feel guilty—am I being selfish because I want her back but on my own terms? The only alternatives are to throw the whole thing away, or to live with this awkward, weird, close/not-close thing.

In these situations, should you say something? When faced with a deteriorating friendship where you know what the problem is but you're not sure how to say it and you don't think they'll be able to change, consider the following:

Was this quality always there? The more it's always been a part of them and the older they are, the less realistic it is that they'll change.

Do they have insight into themselves? A person who doesn't have a clue as to how she is coming across to other people—and has a ton of defenses but so much as a smidgen of acknowledgment about them—is probably not going to take the discussion well.

How compartmentalized is this issue in their personality? In the case of Latisha's friend, anything having to do with child rearing was cause for stressful interactions. Realistically, that topic would not go away as a source of discussion anytime soon. It's easier to avoid the problem when someone gets insufferable only around election time or when paying a bill at a restaurant. But in cases where the negative qualities are embedded in aspects of daily life, it is much more difficult to escape.

How temporary is it? Can you see a point in the not-so-distant future when this hot-button trait won't be at the forefront of your interactions? If so, you might choose to stick it out. But in Latisha's case, that would mean waiting to be empty nesters—if even then, as we all know that grown children create problems, too!

WHEN CHANGE CAN BE GOOD: LETTING FRIENDSHIPS AGE LIKE WINE RATHER THAN SPROUT FUNGUS LIKE SOUR CREAM

And now you may start to understand why cross-generational friendships can have such benefits! Sometimes not being in the same stage at the same time can relieve a bit of pressure (unless, of course, the older person is a know-it-all about what they've been through). Read on for Georgia's take on the ups and downs of a cross-generational friendship that survived it all:

I met Jen because I babysat her kids; there is almost a twenty-year age difference between us. Before I knew it, I was in college and we would go shopping together and hang out a lot. She was in some ways like a mom or a big sister; I could ask her about things and get somewhat more reliable answers than I would from my friends. But I think she was also try-ing to relive her youth. (I'm now that age—mid-thirties—that she was when we met, and I'm definitely much more vain about my age than I ever was.) We did and still do love each other; it's almost like a family relationship.

We had our problems. We didn't talk for a few years when I really felt like growing up a bit and saw her as not being so responsible for her age. And then randomly one day she called, and we started talking again. And now I wouldn't say that we're exactly back to where we were. (I used to think the sun rose and set on her.) But we're friends again. We still talk on the phone, and if I'm on the West Coast, I see her. I know that I could still count on her. She's a part of my life like family.

And sometimes, a friendship that hit an even rougher patch can be redeemed. Though some of us would never again want to lay eyes on our high school nemesis, there can indeed be a happy ending—such as in Callie's story:

Toni and I were inseparable for two years in high school. We were both dealing with upheaval in our home lives; plus, we were both pretty insecure teenage girls who worried about our weight, our appearance, and our social lives. It was one of those friendships that developed almost to the exclu-sion of other people.

However, as time went on, Toni gathered a new circle of friends around her. And everything changed one day my junior year. I arrived at my small, private girls' school to find no one would speak to me. The girls who had been my friends the day before were ignoring me. And worst of all, Toni was the cause of it. She had simply decided that she was done with me and had convinced everyone around us that I was no longer part of their group.

What followed was very tough. For over a year, I struggled to find a place to be and friends to spend time with. All the while, I never really understood why Toni had done this to me. It wasn't until I left for college that I really moved on.

Over the years, I thought about her and wondered where she was and hoped she was happy. While she caused me a lot of pain, with a few years behind me, I grew to understand that she was likely in greater pain at the time. Finally, almost two years ago, a mutual friend put us back in touch.

We met up when she was back in town and were able to talk through everything that had happened between us almost twenty years before. As I had suspected, she was really unhappy when we were in high school and I had been the one to receive the brunt of that hurt. While it was good to finally get an apology for a period in my life that had caused me a lot of pain, it was even better to bring a friend back into my life. We have remained in touch, trading photos of our families, talking on Facebook, and getting together when she is back in town. I can honestly say that it gives me great comfort to have resolved this period of my life.

What made this happy ending feasible is that Toni grew up—truly grew up—and took the initiative to understand and apologize for her actions. This isn't merely friending someone on Facebook and assuming that they've gotten over your *Mean Girls*–era snubs—it's about making real amends. Also, there is some luck involved that the two women remained relatively compatible; no one drastically changed their identity, life outlook, or worldview. And Callie had enough insight and maturity to bless her long-ago friend with real forgiveness.

Though long on odds, Toni and Callie's story speaks to the power and possibilities of shared history within a friendship. In this instance, at least, one can even believe that the next phase of that friendship will be much better than the original.

8

WHEN SEX GETS IN THE WAY

*Friendships with Exes, and the Lines
Between Love and That Kind of Love*

A note on terminology:

This chapter discusses sexual and romantic entanglements and their effects on friendship. Due to the tedium and space demands of writing him or her *each time, I usually settle on* him. *But by no means does this imply that the discussion applies only to women, or only to those in heterosexual romances.*

The possible complications within the intersection of sex and friendship are innumerable; where would bad TV shows be otherwise? But some quandaries come up much more frequently than others, and we'll start with one of the most common. Is it kosher, or instead downright odious, to go for a friend's ex?

CAN I GO FOR MY FRIEND'S EX?

Of course, there's no prescription for absolutely everyone. (Though making any moves before your friend has had her triumphant return to the dance floor for "I Will Survive" is always a bad idea.) But here are some considerations:

1. Really. Does it have to be *this* person? Really? Have you had intense feelings for him for a long time, or do

you think you are just reacting to his newfound availability?

2. Are you willing to wait long enough to make sure that he is not rebounding, and that you don't pour even more salt in your friend's wound than necessary?

3. Are you willing to accept the risk of permanently tainting your friendship?

4. Are there any reasons that this person would be an unwise catch (besides the obvious)?

5. Are you certain you're not acting out of some sort of aggression toward your friend?

6. Has this scenario happened before?

7. Are you willing to be honest with your friend and break the news to her like an adult? (If you can't pay this price, the new relationship doesn't sound worth it.)

8. Are you reasonably certain this person is even interested in you?

Again, this can be murky. Some people celebrate their fiftieth wedding anniversary with such a story of how they got together, and the fact that they had to hurt a distant friend's feelings so many years back is the tiniest trickle of water under the bridge. Other times, it's the friendship that would have been the far greater prize, yet it was irrevocably ruined by a ridiculous decision that ended up lasting all of three and a half nights. There is no crystal ball. But as a general rule, don't dare go for a friend's ex unless you have a reasonable belief that that romance will be worth a shattered friendship. Some women may easily get over an ex dating a friend, but others won't. And if you're going to be the new woman, it's a risk you must be okay with taking.

WHEN "LET'S JUST BE FRIENDS" CAN ACTUALLY WORK...

Now, what do you do when the friendship in doubt is one with your actual ex?

It's one of the most clichéd lines of all time (second perhaps only to "Working hard or hardly working?"): "I hope we can still be friends." From press releases acknowledging celebrity divorces to impromptu breakup speeches delivered in front of junior high lockers, there is a notion in our culture that breakups should be sweet and amicable. It's often thought that the best way to end a romantic relationship is to magically embark on a close, happy, friendship—where everyone is thrilled, and both parties smilingly tease each other about his Frappuccino addiction or her fondness for mohair sweaters.

But does this fantasy ever work out, and is it even wise to try for it? Are you really meant to be friends with your ex (even if he does know you better than your sister, your dachsund, and your best girlfriend combined)? Do great—or even terrible—romances end best by segueing into a friendship?

The answer, many times, is no. Instead, often a post-breakup friendship is wrought with more stress and nausea than a Sylvester Stallone movie marathon. In some cases, becoming friends can happen—eventually. But certain conditions must be met. Here are the bare minimum criteria for a chance at "Let's Just Be Friends" actually to come true:

Whatever attraction is or isn't there is pretty much mutual, as was the decision to end the romance. This means there's no drama of one-sided, unrequited sexual tension, where one person is still stinging from the breakup and the other person has three dates for next Thursday. Both of you should also be on the same page about whether or not "Let's just be friends" means hanging out together every weekend or just being particularly pleasant should you bump into each other on the subway.

It is transparent and honest. If you dumped your ex because you really wanted to start seeing Rick from accounting, you can't go embarking on some elaborate ruse to cover that up and still expect to maintain friendship harmony with your ex at the same time. Similarly, if he ended things by saying that he was taking a job in Tucson, a friendship is not going to work out very well if three months later you see him in the drive-through of a local Burger King. There's no real friendship to be had if the foundation of that friendship isn't mostly on the up-and-up.

Of course, you aren't required to give him hourly updates about whom you're interested in, who's interested in you, or whom you flirted with in traffic. Discretion is key when segueing from a sexual to a nonsexual relationship. But if you're spending so much energy covering up something, keeping something from him, or engaging in some sort of sham worthy of an Emmy nomination, you should remember that that's not much of a real friendship anyway. How could the stress of that charade be worth it?

Holding on to the friendship isn't an excuse to stay together romantically. Is it really just friendship you want? If your notion of being friends looks no different from your notion of being romantically involved, then the "friendship" is a friendship in name only—there is none of the trust, openness, or comfort of a real platonic relationship. Plus, expectations and rules aren't clear, and the reason for the breakup hasn't been resolved. If you're both saying that you're just friends when in reality you're still involved, it's the emotional equivalent of a pyrotechnic high-wire act. And it's bound to come crashing down eventually, with my money on you both ending up in flames.

You have more in common than just your romantic past, and there was a true friendship there—or the strong potential for

one—in the first place. Romantic relationships that peter out because you never had anything to talk about are not exactly going to become all-star friendships once the kissing has ended. Make no mistake: If your relationship was the stuff of a music video, with a lot of spark but no actual substance or platonic connection, you are fooling yourself to think that you will suddenly start having the same sense of humor, values, or nonsexual interest in each other. If your relationship had two speeds—silence and bedroom—then chances are, you'll find it awkward, at best, to be sharing coffee and discussing the latest scoop from *The Huffington Post.*

In these cases, the much better option is to "remain friends" in the Hollywood-publicist sense of the phrase, where both of you just take a deep breath, complain to your real friends about how shallow/unworldly/humorless he was, and never have a conversation with each other again.

You are willing to enlarge your circle. A friendship with an ex is *not* healthy when it is fallen into because he's the only person you know in the city, or you're terrified of spending the Fourth of July—or Saint Patrick's Day or the winter solstice—alone. In order to properly transition your ex into the friend category, you've got to make an honest effort to reach out and enlarge your social circle, which includes getting closer to friends you already had and also meeting new people. You can't expect your former love to play the same role in your emotional intimacy as he did when there were other kinds of intimacy as well. If you do, your "friendship" will be incredibly self-destructive and will keep you in a stranglehold. How could you really move on?

The relationship was healthy enough that there are no lasting scars, but not so perfect that it will be idealized forevermore. There is danger here in both directions. Naturally, if your relationship was explosive, and not in a good way, then the residual resentment, hurt, and anger will not disappear just because you're no longer sleeping with each other. To expect that an easy-breezy camaraderie will ensue when the reason you broke up was that you couldn't stop screaming at each other is not only unrealistic but also quite risky. You may very well end up having to deal with a double-whammy breakup: first with the romantic relationship and second with the implosion of your platonic dream.

On the other hand, if your romantic relationship was all daisies, oversized carnival teddy bears, and kisses in the rain, and you broke up only because he wasn't Jewish or you decided to join the Peace Corps, then you run the risk of idealizing your romance. What's the harm, you may ask? Well, it can certainly be hard to move on when you not only have visions of how perfect this guy was for you, but when he's also still in your life, texting you—or even your mom—when a birthday rolls around. That's not the type of situation a potential new boyfriend will appreciate.

DANGER, WILL ROBINSON: WHEN IT ABSOLUTELY POSITIVELY CANNOT WORK

So you think you passed that test, huh? You and your ex are going to keep each other as each other's emergency contacts and perhaps even shop for BFF lockets? Well, don't be so sure. There are some dealbreakers—situations where it cannot work, even if all the other criteria are met—that you should be aware of.

One of you really means the friendship thing, and the other is just using it as the breakup buzzword du jour and has no interest in being friends. One word: *pain.* And lots of it. Needless to say (though I'm going to anyway), consistent pain has no place in a friendship—unless you do each other's bikini waxes.

There is no mutual respect. If you were constantly belittling each other during your relationship or you don't truly think he's all that great a human being, then being in a friendship together will be an exercise in sadism. (And not the sexy kind!)

There was emotional (or other!) abuse during the relationship.
If one or both people were engaged in any kind of deliberate or even
semi-deliberate harm toward the other, this has no place in a friendship. Ask yourself honestly if you can really imagine this person
treating you right, or if you instead are caught in an extremely dangerous cycle of feeling like you need to have the person close to you
in order to survive, and then letting them hurt you. This can be serious, and if you're in this situation, it's not a bad idea to think about
getting some professional support. There are more details about
what professional help is out there in chapter 11.

***One or both of you would be extremely jealous to see the other
meeting someone new.*** This is the reality of why friendships after a
breakup, at least for the first year, are often not a great idea. Would
you honestly be okay with hearing the guy whom you used to
think was the "one" talking excitedly about some awesome new
intern named Emily? Why put yourself through that? Conversely,
how comfortable is it for you to keep the friendship banter light
and fluffy when you would rather be excitedly blathering on about
what a great kiss you had last night with this new dude Raoul?

***You have not yet given each other space to let the romantic
relationship die.*** Even if all other signs point toward the possibility of a really wonderful friend relationship, you still need a
cooling-off period. No breakup is completely amicable. Period. It's
virtually impossible to have been romantically entangled with someone and not have a few feelings get bruised on the way out. This is
true even if it was a completely mutual decision, or if you were the
one who dumped him. And the various emotions that are running
through your body the first few weeks of a breakup—some hybrid
of sadness and fear, with a good helping of affection starvation
thrown in—are not the most stable of platforms on which to build
a friendship. Give yourself time to let the aftershocks of the breakup
wear off. You've got to return to who you are as an individual, rather

than who you are as part of a couple, before deciding whether or not you really want to keep some connection going.

WHEN FRIENDS HATE YOUR BOYFRIEND: YOUR JOB AS REFEREE

It happens to many of us at some point: You're dating someone new, and while you were hoping that your friends would think your significant other is the greatest thing since sliced bread (have you seen how if he squints a certain way, he looks like Don Draper?), instead they seem to feel he's the equivalent of long-since-molded French toast. What did you do wrong? Do they really think your taste is bad? Are they jealous? Can't they just butt out? Will they bust out the posterboard picket signs, develop some snazzy chant, and hold a protest at your future wedding?

There's no reason to panic. Sometimes what seems like disapproval is just noncommitment. Maybe they don't want to gush over someone you've barely had a fourth date with; maybe they're unsure how you really feel about the guy. Maybe they're used to you changing your mind often, and they don't want to be on record as stating that yes, they like his eyelashes. Maybe they *are* jealous, or maybe you're caught up so much in your new relationship excitement that you've neglected to ask them how that new job is going or how their sister is doing after her surgery. Perhaps you're so infatuated right now that any response from them—short of physical swooning in your new man's presence—is bound to look like not enough.

And there also is the more disturbing possibility that you have chosen someone subpar, or even subhuman. If you value your friends' opinions, have no rational reason to suspect that they have ulterior motives, and are willing to make yourself open to what they have to say without holding a grudge, then you can gently initiate a conversation about why they seem to be less than enthused about your new man. Try to take their feedback seriously without letting it matter more than your own instincts. Part of being a good friend is giving and taking feedback while incorporating it into what your gut tells you to do. You should be neither a pushover nor a block-it-outer when it comes to your friends' opinions. Sometimes, that means that you'll make some mistakes. And it's best if you've shown enough respect to your friends that they'll still want to be there when things come crashing down. (If you're on the other side of the equation—and are in total disapproval of your friend's romantic partner—you'll want to see chapter 6.)

LET ME JUST *GO* BRUSH MY TEETH AND FREAK *OUT*: POST-HOOKUP DAMAGE CONTROL

So it happened. Blame the moonlight, blame the open bar. Blame boredom, loneliness, or even Barry White. But you hooked up with someone who was a platonic friend, and now you're alternately confused, horrified, and wondering how the heck you never noticed his extremely large amount (it's virtually a forest!) of neck hair.

1. First, don't panic.

Don't do anything further you'll regret. This means you should stop, right there, in your tracks. As much as you might be tempted to call it a huge mistake or, alternatively, tell him that it was the best night of your life, *halt*. The morning after should never contain any grand pronouncements one way or the other. You need time to figure things out, and you don't want to say something that you'll feel differently about when you actually have your underwear on.

2. Treat the person with respect.

Regardless of how you feel about it, this is no time to turn into Bad Cop. Some of the feelings you *do* have about the situation—shame, embarrassment, fear, confusion, regret—might tempt you to take out all your discomfort on him, the Dude Who's Now Using Your

Shower. Resist the notion. Leaving a bitter taste in the other person's mouth won't do you any good in the long run.

Give yourself some time to figure out why this happened. Just as you don't have to decide exactly how you feel about it right away, you also don't have to point fingers at him or blame yourself. By all means, though, if you have an uneasy feeling that you were taken advantage of, don't stuff those feelings. Give yourself some time and space, alone, to sort through the hows, whys, and whats.

3. Don't tell too many people.

The situation may be humorous. It may be horrifying. (Or it may be humorous *and* horrifying, sort of like *Borat*.) But resist the urge to share the gory details—or even a plot summary—with anyone whom you wouldn't trust with planning your funeral, at least not until you've thought it through completely. (This means no cryptic, begging-for-attention Tweets, either!)

4. Do address any health issues.

The effects of a one-night stand, even with someone you trust, can be more than mental. If you have any concerns about a lack of protection or contraception, deal with them pronto by scheduling an appointment with a doctor.

5. Do look for larger patterns with other men and/or women.

When you get down to thinking about this, be honest with yourself if it's happening too often, or if it's indicative of a larger problem with alcohol, self-esteem, boundary violations, or sex. Often what looks like a fluky mistake can be part of a larger pattern that is worth paying attention to.

6. Do try to be honest with yourself about whether you might be harboring feelings for the person.

Even though it's easy to blame all other circumstances, we don't have to be in some gooey romance novel for the possibility to exist that you have feelings for this person. Don't be so busy berating yourself that you drive yourself into denial. It's certainly not the Jane Austen way of courtship, but there might be a budding romance in there after all.

After a couple of days, perhaps consisting of house arrest, a pint of mango sorbet, and a crisis summit with your closest friends who are *not* him, you can then decide how you want to proceed. Of course, it's certainly a popular choice to try to ignore the whole thing and pretend that nothing happened, and take cues from him. (More on how that might turn out in a minute.)

Addressing the One-Night Stand

If you do want to address the fling, there are a few guidelines to keep in mind.

- *Be careful with your terminology. Don't insult him OR yourself.*
- *Be discreet. Don't e-mail it, text it, Tweet it, or singing-telegram it (those get expensive).*
- *Be gentle but not ambiguous.*
  If you know that you regret this and you wish you could erase it altogether, don't give him false hope (or fear!) that you ever want to repeat it. But don't make him feel worse.
- *Realize that doing nothing might have more consequences than doing something.*

Again, many people are tempted to pretend that nothing happened. They hope and expect to slide back into purely platonic camaraderie, or signing off on each other's time sheets, without issue. But often it's the unresolved tension or awkwardness that kills a friendship. Or the reality that for one person, it meant something, and for another, it didn't.

This is actually one of the biggest risks of a hookup among two friends: What are the chances that you're both really on the same page? Frequently, the friendship collapses because someone is hung up on the other. Hookups don't happen in a vacuum. With all the variability between the two of you in how you might be feeling, it's hard to predict whether your friendship will survive. Sometimes, especially when feelings are involved that are one-sided, it most certainly can't.

UNREQUITED LOVE: WHEN "JUST FRIENDS" ISN'T ENOUGH FOR ONE OF YOU

Where would the film industry be without the notion of unrequited love? Romantic comedies, dramas, and even awfully gory horror films have long capitalized on the fact that just because you love someone, there's no guarantee they'll love you back. (Or even respond to your nineteenth fan letter about how much they rocked in *Dancing with the Stars*.)

So you're friends with someone, but you really want to be more. Maybe you already share dinners together, but you'd love for there to be cloth napkins and candlelight instead of peanuts and straw dispensers. Maybe you share laughs and confidences, but noogies and high fives are the extent of the physical action.

Do you make your move—and risk jeopardizing the friendship? Or do you suffer in silence, hoping that either your feelings will diminish or theirs will become clear?

A few general considerations:

What's the weight of your feelings versus the weight of your friendship? Do you tend to have crushes on a lot of people? Do you go through this frequently with those you admire? Do you have reason to suspect that your feelings will pass?

Also, how important and long-standing is your friendship? If you don't have much history with this person, and you're convinced that you see them as a potential date and not much else, then you're not risking as much by going for the romantic gold. On the other hand, if you can't possibly imagine not having this person in your life, but you're pretty sure that you'll get over not dating them fairly quickly, it may be best to try to nip those sparks in the bud.

How one-sided is it? You can never be completely impartial about this, but you might have a decent idea. Try your hardest to be objective. Are you too modest—he's flirting, too, and you're missing it because you don't want to get your hopes up? Or, is he pretty clearly not into you and instead you're thinking he's about to buy you jewelry? You must acknowledge, honestly, how you tend to view these sorts of situations and if you have an inflated or deflated sense of what's going on. A mutual friend might come in handy for giving you the score. (Though I wouldn't advise her to follow you two around with a video camera and a clipboard.)

Can you hedge your bets and make a move without really doing so? There might be an opportunity when you can volley the ball so subtly—a certain half-flirty innuendo, an overly playful invitation—that you are able to give him an opportunity to send you a signal while you get to save major face if your semi-pass is not acted upon.

How sensitive and subtle is this person capable of being? If he were to reject an advance, would he turn it into a federal matter? Is he the type to automatically make you feel more awkward than necessary? Or could you see him respecting and sparing your feelings, refusing to make a bad situation worse? The office loudmouth, for instance, might not be that likely to keep your embarrassment from growing exponentially.

How would you really react to the idea that your friendship was totally over? Vegas pawnbrokers can tell you: If you're going to risk losing something, you've got to have an honest assessment of its value. Think worst-case scenario. Assuming that things were to explode in a fiery inferno, or simmer in a stew of awkwardness for the next several months until you gradually can't stand to make eye contact anymore, how devastated would you be?

To sum up, here's a final test. What feels more like a kick in the gut: the idea that five years from now, you never went for it and yet he was in love with you all along but finally moved on or the idea that five years from now, your friendship has long since disintegrated due to the awkwardness of your late-night attempt at a striptease?

Of course, many times it's not you whom the feelings are coming from—it's them, as Kara learned:

I dated this guy for four years—and was tight with his group of friends, including Pat. For what seemed like forever, Pat's and my friendship progressed normally. Then one night everyone went out for something, leaving us alone. We were watching a movie when we started wrestling or something, I honestly can't remember. I ended up on top of him on this chair and there was an honest-to-God moment of electricity between us. I leapt off of him and we didn't mention the incident. A year later, I had broken up with that loser boyfriend and had started dating this guy Chad. I went home one weekend to visit Pat and some old friends. Pat was acting weird; I asked him what was wrong.

He started crying and asked me if I remembered that night at his house. I was stunned: clearly it affected him more than I imagined. So he admits that he's had this thing for me forever and can't stand that I'm seeing someone else. We eventually kiss. I felt guilty because (1) I just didn't feel that way about him and (2) I was technically seeing someone else at the time. I left after that. It didn't take long before our friendship completely collapsed. He came up to see me and nearly started a fight with Chad because he couldn't stand to see me with him. (Mature, right?) We never really talked again. I hope at least he's happy. It definitely sucked to lose a friend.

While Kara was clueless about the depth of Pat's feelings until long after the wrestling-match-with-electricity, other times you might be tempted to aid and abet the situation, even when you know it's not good for either of you. Here's what Stephanie went through:

I had broken up with my long-term boyfriend, and I used Jay as a stand-in boyfriend. Whenever we got together with our friends, I would sit with him, put his arms around me, hold his hand, and we would be physically close. I would also tell him all my problems and lean on him in that way, as a source of comfort.

I told myself he should know I wasn't interested in being more than friends, and since he was friends with my ex, I figured he would think taking things further was off-limits anyway.

I knew deep down that I was justifying how I was acting because I didn't want to feel alone. I was attracted to having someone care about me and be there when I needed some-one. And I admit when in the presence of my ex, I wanted to hurt him by having him see me with Jay. Later on, after graduation, Jay and I hooked up—once. I left in the middle of that and finally started putting more distance between us. It really wasn't until I met my current husband that I started sensing Jay was upset by my relationship. And I finally figured out that I had probably hurt him more than I realized. Then he didn't RSVP to my wedding, and we didn't have contact for about five years. Just last year he friended me on Facebook, and we've had a few superficial contacts with each other. I wish I had not let the affection escalate. I knew I was never going to be interested in more, and he was such a great guy and a great friend. I really regret damaging that friendship.

In both these cases, it was easy for the women to fool themselves into thinking that a little bit of physical affection could be forgotten. But in reality, it was indicative of—and a catalyst to—a much bigger desire on the parts of their friends. Giving in to that physical moment was the downfall of both friendships. Indeed, unrequited love has killed many friendships, whether there are actual hookups or not. And though the popular stereotype would say that this is more likely to happen with a woman pining for her male friend, clearly those examples show that it can—and does—work in different ways. In fact, in a story that also brings to mind the perils of technology (flashback to chapter 3!) we see another example, from *Knit and Tonic* blogger Wendy Bernard:

It was the mid-'90s, and we had just started having e-mail in the office. A friend of mine would come over and I'd cut her hair, we'd have a glass of wine and hang out. I had a boyfriend, but she once tried to kiss me. I said, "Becky, come on now, you know I'm not interested in you that way." She got really, really offended at how I handled it, and was mad at me. I tried to apologize to her, brought her some tomatoes from my garden, but she kept saying how embarrassed she was. Then she sent me a really nasty e-mail, and I wrote back, "Well, I love you, too!"—a sarcastic dig. But she came walking over to my cubicle with a smile and googly eyes—I put two and two together. She thought I was serious and that I loved her!

Though perhaps a story to chuckle about now, the loss of more serious friendships can still be painful years later. It can be hard to wonder what might have been, and as the first two stories indicate, it can lead to much regret.

Other times, people have wonderful friendship chemistry that is mistaken for romantic chemistry and leads to embarking on an actual, ill-fated romantic relationship that can also lead to years of remorse. Says Keisha:

I met Jeff at work, and we ended up at this party, had a lot to drink, and connected. It turned into something romantic.

All through the relationship, even when it was going south, we always said we should have stayed just friends. We should never have crossed the line. But we got so entangled. There were so many definite red flags that we weren't compatible in a relationship. Part of it was immaturity and lack of experience. But much of it was not being able to draw the line between someone being good for you as a friend and good for you as a partner. But we kind of cocooned at that party and didn't come out of that cocoon for five years. For four years we lived together. I lost most of my friends that I had when I met him. At that first party, yes, there was a meaningful connection, but that's different from something that has to become physical. Then heavy-duty dating, heavy-duty exclusivity, heavy-duty engagement. That was a mistake, and our relationship went bad.

But he had a pull over me, and that pull was really a friendship. To this day, I miss him as a friend. There are times that I think how great it'd be to have his perspective. There were certain conversations I would have with him that I can't have anymore. It really made me cautious about crossing the line with someone because you really lose something if the relationship doesn't work out. If we had not taken that step at the party, we'd still be friends to this day. There was nothing about our romantic relationship that was worth sacrificing the friendship for. You hear about those relationships where someone says, "At least I had the dance." In this case, the dance was not worth it! "It's better to have loved and lost. . . ." Well, not always. I lost a real friendship.

So, as for the decision whether to let a friendship become something more, that's all the calculations I can offer you without resorting to advanced trigonometry. Either way—going for it or doing nothing—is a risk, but the upshot is that either way could also be turned into a winning situation—it's all within your control. It's not just how he responds; it's also how you spin it.

WHEN IT'S BAD

So you feel like the protagonist in a '50s girl-band song because you went for it and it didn't happen. Or maybe you're so certain he's not into you "that way" that you've decided to simmer in silence, with things feeling just as painful and awkward as if you'd hired a singing telegram to declare your undying love for his dimples. Either way, you've got a challenge ahead: How do you attempt to salvage the friendship when your heart is beating overtime?

First, decide if the friendship is worth salvaging. Often, the idea of staying friends feels pleasing because it's an opportunity to stay close to the person and therefore smell them, see their smile, and keep close tabs on whom they might start to date. (That bitch!) But make sure the practical day-to-day aspects of the friendship are actually fulfilling to you in a way that is independent of your romantic feelings. Don't hang on to being friends simply because you can't imagine being without him—you've really got to reevaluate if you'll get anything out of the friendship other than frustration, pain, or gastrointestinal distress worthy of a twenty-ninth bean burrito.

Examine your motivations. Would keeping him in your life platonically really add something? Could you get over your jealousy when he does date someone and truly have his best interests at heart? Would it be bad for your self-esteem to be reminded constantly that nothing's going to happen romantically? Might you end up overly scrutinizing your appearance, the jokes you tell, or the way that you sit in what may just amount to the psychological equivalent of a never-ending, one-sided first date? Are you going through what really amounts to self-torture: entertaining some fancy that he might change his mind?

Some people end up realizing that the friendship itself was something of a sham: a flimsy bridge that attempted to move things forward romantically. And they must admit that when that prospect is gone, they're really not interested in hearing about his annoying boss anymore. (Why doesn't he just quit already?) What used to be titillating now becomes at best, boring, and at worst, excruciating. At this point, you may choose to bow out gracefully and subtly.

Other people really are interested in maintaining the friendship and are capable of putting aside their bruised egos. This might be helped by the type of cognitive dissonance that often accompanies rejection. ("Well, thank goodness—I'm too good for him anyway."

"It's probably best that we don't get involved." "I would eventually have gotten *so* grossed out by all that back acne.")

Another consideration is whether something about your unrequited love dynamic was what was keeping the friendship alive in the first place. Perhaps your crush, regardless of why he couldn't be with you, was energized by your interest in him (whether you officially spilled it to him or not). Be prepared that even if you are successful in no longer being attracted to him—all those visualizations of his toenails helped—this does not necessarily spell success. Your friendship may end up falling flat without the spark of the old attraction, no matter how one-sided and painful it was.

In summation, when you're at the bad end of unrequited love and wondering whether you can stomach a friendship, here's a plan of action:

1. Give yourself some time and space to decide if you truly want to keep the friendship going.

2. Don't fall into the temptation of still trying to put on an attractive show for him. *(It's natural to look in the mirror an extra time, but don't even think of wearing the new Jimmy Choos to kickball!)*

3. Don't dwell on your feelings; try to give up the fantasy.

Be honest with yourself about your feelings. But don't ruminate to the point where every time you see him your reaction becomes a reaction *about* your reaction. You can overthink this to the point of misery. Giving up the thought of being together is perhaps the hardest part of this whole process, but eventually, you've got to stop indulging your fantasies. (Yes, that kind, too!)

4. Try to detect if he's playing with your feelings.

It's a ghastly thought that your unattainable Prince Charming might not have your best interests at heart, but some people just love being wanted. Don't let yourself be played. If your friendship is determined to move on in a platonic direction, his messing with you will do nothing for the cause, and instead take your emotional health as a prisoner.

5. Shift your activities to be absolutely, positively platonic.

It's simple: if you're eventually going to nip the romantic feelings in the bud, having drinks together in a dim, smoky room is not going to facilitate that process.

6. Observe yourself with him and try to be honest if you are being yourself and are happy with how you're behaving.

You need not have an out-of-body experience, but you must increase your awareness of how you're behaving in the moment. Just as with the rules of "regular" friendship, you must make sure that you're not turning into someone you don't want to be.

7. Prepare yourself for the inevitable "he's seeing someone," but don't dwell.

I hate to be the one to say it, but yes, he'll see someone someday. She might even be a Heidi Klum look-alike brain surgeon who crochets afghans for orphanages with one hand while editing her sellout stand-up comedy act with the other. Denying this possibility won't help matters. Instead, know that the sooner you help yourself move on, the more likely you'll be dating your own version of awesomeness by the time that day rolls around.

8. Expand your interests and start looking for other people, but not to make him jealous.

Going out with your mutual friend Harry, who is about as interesting as a nosebleed, is not going to do anyone any good. And no, it won't make your crush jealous.

9. Go ahead and do it: make a list of reasons why you're not compatible.

Keep your cognitive defenses strong. At the very least, there's the harsh reality that if he's not into you enough to make things work, then that would be the absolute worst kind of relationship to be in.

FOOLING YOURSELF: WHEN YOU'RE THINKING "JUST FRIENDS," BUT YOU'RE ACTUALLY HAVING AN AFFAIR

Sometimes, the challenge exists in the opposite direction. You desperately want to convince yourself that you're "just friends" with someone because one or both of you are otherwise involved, but in reality there's more to it. Technological advances have greatly increased the possibility of this. The Internet (chapter 3 again!) gives us the ability to connect and reconnect with someone instantaneously and effortlessly, and it lets us carefully portray ourselves in the most attractive light, with the best possible pictures (that dress is smokin'!) and the most carefully chosen words (no one will know I spent forty minutes on that status update!). A study released by Divorce-Online in early 2010 suggested that one in five divorce filings specifically mentions Facebook, with the most common problem cited being an affair developing through the social networking site. The risk of falling into an emotional—or physical—affair with someone who is supposedly just a friend is arguably greater than ever before.

Signs Your "Friendship" Is Moving into Something Riskier

At what point is an online friendship something to be concerned about? Where is the line drawn between a harmless or even beneficial friendship and an emotional affair? The entire issue exists on a continuum, but, as always, I've got some considerations for you. If you or the friend in question is in a committed relationship with someone else, the following will help you figure out if your "friendship" may be moving into dangerous territory:

- Are you tempted to keep your contact secret because your partner "wouldn't understand"?
- Are you overly concerned with crafting the image that you portray to this person?
- Do you find yourself sharing confidences with this person that you wouldn't—or couldn't—share with your partner?
- Do you find yourself comparing this person to your partner—even just in your head—and putting your partner in a negative light?
- Do you find yourself getting a little too excited to get a message from, or see, this person?
- Has the talk gotten racy or significantly flirtatious?
- Do you find yourself getting jealous of this person's partner?
- Have you noticed that the more frustrated or bored you are with your partner, the more contact you have with this person?
- Do you find yourself wanting this person to be attracted to you, even if you convince yourself that you're not attracted to him or her?
- Do you have an idealized notion of this person?
- Do you make excuses for your relationship with this person or even blame it on your partner?
- Have you tried to set limits and had difficulty doing so?
- Have you seen a progression in the intensity of your thoughts about the relationship?

This isn't black-and-white, as there's no such thing as emotional litmus paper. (Though it would surely make my job easier!) But you must listen to your gut. Answering yes to any of these questions is something to think about, and the more yeses, the more cause for concern. "Friendship" can easily mask a burgeoning affair, and it's easy to be in denial about the nature of your relationship, especially when you're committed to someone else.

Complicating things further, the spark of reconnecting with someone, even platonically, can sometimes be stimulating in a way that is difficult to distinguish from romantic excitement. But if the rush that you feel when your old crush Joe sends a message has *nothing* in common with the excitement you felt when you located your third-grade neighbor Monica, then you need to be honest with yourself.

It's Gone Too Far—How Do You Deal?

To move in the direction of salvaging your original relationship:

1. Have a day of reckoning, and cut out the denial.
2. Look for deeper meaning. What might this reveal about your relationship? Or you?
3. Cut it off. Be brief and decisive in stopping the connection. Give yourself logistical support in doing so, whether by defriending the person, blocking their instant messages, deleting their number from your cell phone, or trashing their e-mails without reading them.
4. Reestablish a connection with your partner. Address the issues that led to this disconnect, by counseling if need be. Clarify your commitment and renew it (not with an Elvis impersonator, but with new energy, focus, and intent toward reestablishing intimacy).

Often, the attraction to someone else is symptomatic of challenges in the original relationship. Says Aimee:

Ted and I have been together for ten years now, entirely in peaks and valleys. Love is there, no doubt, but he has always had a temper that kept things on edge, and I was often the recipient of the downside of his mood. For years I told him he should talk to someone, get his anger and sadness in check. He never did. Despite this, we continued down the "normal" path of marriage and kids—something we both wanted, but sometimes I wonder if these issues should have been dealt with first. After our first child, things got worse. His mood was always down, and he just didn't pay attention to me at all. Eventually, I just couldn't take it, and around then, my boss and I had become good friends. He's older than me, but at the same place in life regarding marriage and kids. We would sit and talk and found friendship, something I had been severely lacking for a long time. I started looking at him with a different set of eyes throughout that month. I really began to look forward to seeing him every day. I would think of my silly crush and how I took the extra effort to look nice; I hadn't been this lighthearted in years. I never imagined he felt the same.

One day at lunch, we were sitting across from each other and you could feel the sparks between us. I was going insane; it was so intense. I just took a deep breath and walked back to my office. Well, he followed. And that line was crossed. And continued to be crossed over the next couple of weeks. Yes, I knew it was wrong. But I didn't care. I felt needed and wanted and enjoyed for the first time in so long. I had no idea until then that he was going through the same thing in his own marriage. We were two lost souls who happened to find each other at the right (or wrong) time. Ted noticed something, and we had it out. I don't think he realized until that night how far he—and we—had slipped. He promised to get therapy; I agreed, for our child's sake. It was a long, heartbreaking, sleepless, tearful night. I went to work the next morning and told my friend (ha!) what had happened. He was concerned, for me and himself. The aftermath was the hardest year of my life, going to marriage counseling, dealing with my feelings for my work buddy—who was into me, too, a lot. We were emotionally involved with each other on a level that we shouldn't have been. We're strictly friends now; it's actually liberating. In another time, another life, maybe something else. Things at home are still peaks and valleys. Therapy and meds did wonders for Ted and his depression. But I recognize it's an ongoing battle. Yet I still can't see us splitting—maybe we should, but I don't see it.

Chemistry between people is a peculiar thing. There's no doubt that romantic relationships require a certain kind of chemistry, but friendships do as well. And so it's hard to navigate the overlap that can occasionally develop between the two. But as these stories and guidelines show, examining your motivations, being honest (at least to yourself!) about your feelings, and treating people with respect are those most basic behaviors that can lay the foundation to making sure your friendships and romantic relationships remain as healthy as possible. Even if there are flulike symptoms every once in a while.

9

FAMILY FRIENDS, FAMILY AS FRIENDS, AND FRIENDS AS FAMILY

How to Navigate the Ties That Bind Without Being Bound

You didn't choose them. For some of us, our families of origin have, at best, not much in common with us, and at worst, really negative strongholds on our psyche. Maybe your mother was more Betty Boop than Betty Crocker, or your siblings were about as supportive as a bookcase made of Jell-O. Thank goodness for the fact that there is a family we can choose when the original one is a bit negligent in giving us all we need. This new family is made up of our friends.

WHAT FRIENDS ADD TO THE FAMILY TREE

As the average age of marriage rises in many countries, the United States included, a new attitude is developing about the potential role that adult friends can play in your life. No longer is it a sign of spinsterhood to be spending Thanksgiving at age thirty with your friends passing the rosemary-infused, prosciutto-wrapped pear spears instead of some toddlers poking their fingers into the harriedly mashed potatoes. No longer is it unusual for young adults to take huge, expensive vacations with friends; many do this even after they've long been paired up into romantic relationships.

Pop culture has embraced this with gusto, of course. From *Seinfeld* and *Friends* to *Sex and the City* and *How I Met Your Mother*, there have been plenty of modern depictions of circles of friends becoming like family. And so much can be gained by letting your friends take on a more family-like role in your life, even if your "real" family is fulfilling and healthy. Why reserve that special circle of intimacy just for people who share your surname or your ski jump nose?

For people who have emotional needs that are not met by their families, developing a more family-like relationship with outside friends can be downright healing. There's a special comfort that comes from knowing you don't always have to wear, say, or do the right thing; friends-as-family will love you for your flaws, not in spite of them. It's unconditional, full of trust and a sense of permanence. They know your history enough to laugh at that inside joke from four years ago, and to help you remember your strengths and vulnerabilities. They know what you really want when you're stressed out, and they can call you on your BS when you're fooling even yourself.

There's an emotional intimacy that comes from being with people who are the closest of the close in your circle. At the risk of channeling *The Lion King,* you can feel the love. Being around people who really care about you—really, really care about you, and not because of your position at work or your collection of cashmere or the fact that you have free ski passes—can be uplifting in the worst of times and downright sublime in the best of times. Showing someone that you accept and appreciate them for who they really are is one of the most psychologically beneficial gifts that human beings can offer each other: it's validation in its highest form. This doesn't come just from your happy hour partners or your coworkers or the crew you go to concerts with. Instead, it's your friends-as-family who can make you feel something resembling whole.

THANKSGIVING TAKEOUT IN YOUR APARTMENT: MAKING A FAMILY OUT OF YOUR FRIENDS

How do you take your relationships to this level? First, it takes time—and a lot of it. (No use in putting "Turn Candace into a sister for life!" into your day planner for tomorrow.) Sometimes it will happen without any effort; the years will exert their influence, and shared dramas, comedies, and tragedies will gradually cement the bond to the point of an automatic, comfortable intimacy. But this comes more naturally for some than others. Affectionate, sentimental, let's-do-nothing-but-talk-of-our-feelings types may be prone to developing these best-of-the-best friendships within a few months. For other people, it's easy to feel alone, as if your friends don't get the "real you," or that you don't have someone whom you could call at 3 A.M. with an emotional emergency. Here are some tips to take a close friendship to a more "family" place:

Develop holiday connections with each other. You can even start some new traditions of your own. It doesn't matter if you'll be together on the official day itself: Who says that Kristi and Sophie's Annual Mad-Dash Christmas Gift List Checkoff isn't a tradition that can live on forever?

Embrace domesticity. Do things that will increase the amount of comfort you feel in each other's homes. Focus more on hanging out than planning specific outings. Let her see you in your sweats; don't always feel the need to clean the dishes before she comes over. Let your hair down a bit and enjoy the relaxation that comes from feeling less like a hostess and more like a sister.

Commit yourself. No, not with BFF lockets, but with keys to each other's house, status as plant-waterer permanently on retainer, or that trip to Costa Rica. Making concrete plans to be part of each other's futures helps strengthen the foundation of your friendship, and having responsibility for some aspect of someone's life can actually feel pretty sweet. Moreover, seeing each other in different environs—and having an adventure you can talk about for years to come—can often take a friendship to a higher level.

Blend your legal families. There's got to be someone in your "real" family that you like—no matter how distant or ambiguously related. And the more they get to know your friends, the more your friends can become like family. Let their presence help bring your friends even closer into the fold.

Make it official. Often, having someone play a formal role in a life transition, whether as a godparent to your children, an attendant in your wedding, or the person your master's thesis is dedicated to, can help "legitimize" your relationship.

Trust them with that secret. Yes, I mean that deep, dark secret that you always worried that someone would judge you about. If you've found someone who appears to love you unconditionally, releasing something about yourself that you've never told anyone can lift a weight off your shoulders while also increasing the trust that you both have for each other.

Don't ever be a fair-weather fan. Remember their birthday, each and every year. And if you're late, do it anyway, with an extra apology. Call to support them when their grandma is in the hospital—and remember her name and the reason she's there.

The trick is to continue to think in these terms about your friends even when you might add others to your official, "real" family. Often, people feel like they have to push someone away when they take in someone new (like a committed romantic partner). It's true that you'll probably gossip less about your sex life once you're in a serious relationship, and you'll probably watch more late-night movies with your significant other than with your old girlfriends, but by thinking of your closest friends in the way that you would think about your family, you'll make sure to continue to carve out structured time for them. And the mutual trust that you'll always be in each other's lives will enrich the relationship in the meantime.

It's also important to think in the other direction, not just turning our friends into our family, but making sure that we maximize the ability of our family to become our real friends. Many people struggle with their family relationships; you don't have to have watched *Jerry Springer* to know that family can often equal drama. Thankfully, the real-life dramas are usually more subtle than the *Springer*-esque brawls involving splintered chairs, a tattooed bouncer, and broken noses. But many times they're dysfunctional enough to cause discomfort and dissatisfaction on both sides.

YOUR MOM STiLL CALLS HER "THAT CHRiSTiNE": WHEN FAMiLY AND FRiENDSHiPS DON'T BLEND SO WELL

The mixing of friends and family itself can sometimes create the thorniest dilemmas. But luckily, there are answers. Here is a guide for some of the most common issues. (Yes, the psychologist has seen it all.)

Issue: Your family is disrespectful of boundaries.

Perhaps you find it difficult to let anyone in your life—platonically or romantically—without the approval of your family. Your father has read every one of your leases, and your mother has sounded off on every one of your bras (though she was right about the racerback). Point is, you need to recognize where your life begins and your family's role in it ends. This battle can be fought gradually by asserting yourself with new day-to-day boundaries that you decide in advance. (Maybe it's a daily phone call limit, or not talking about the new person you're seeing until you've had a fourth date, or refusing to answer certain questions and sticking to it.)

Issue: Your family has differing expectations than you do in terms of what your relationships should be like.

Expectations that are never spoken but are worlds apart are going to continue to chafe under the surface until they're dealt with. If one of you doesn't think a card is enough for a sister's birthday, or the other is resentful that her live-in partner is never part of the family Christmas photos, these resentments can simmer year after year. The best way to deal? Be open and respectful in your communication about what you'd like to see, and try to see where the other person is coming from. Only then can you work on a compromise that improves things for both of you. It certainly beats suffering in silence.

Issue: Your family would actually be your best friends, but distance has gotten in the way.

There's a benefit to technology that goes far beyond easy access to developing a fetish for galoshes. Webcams, texting, social networking sites, and blogs have all given us the opportunity to stay a bit closer; it's up to you to do the rest. Pay special attention to chapters 3 and 7 for tips on letting technology help the heart grow fonder during an absence.

Issue: There's been an incident that created a rift that no one wants to bridge.

Life can often be defined by its little moments, those inexplicable, often unpredictable events that permanently shift the direction of relationships. Some of these are good, like when that woman who happened to move in next door to you became your best friend for life, or when your brother broke his leg and came to crash in your apartment and the two of you started talking a lot more. But all too often, they can be bad: your stepsister took something of yours without asking, broke it, lied about it, and it's been chilly ever since.

Your mom hated your college boyfriend and started a smear campaign against him, and you've never forgiven her, even though that guy is history.

If you've got a gap that you want to bridge, it will probably involve making the first move. A well-planned letter that acknowledges your role in the problem and your goal of moving forward can jump-start the process. Just don't expect that both of you will ever be on exactly the same page. You might need to let some things go and start fresh in the interest of progress, even if you didn't get the exact apology or acknowledgment you were hoping for.

Issue: Your family is caught in the inertia of old, unhealthy patterns (sibling rivalries, resentment, disapproval, secrets).

Maybe it's not a particular incident affecting all of you but a bad dynamic that's never been corrected. You simply don't know how to open up to your parents without feeling annoyed; you don't remember how it is to have a conversation with your brother without ragging on him. This takes breaking up your interactions on a micro level and examining your motivations and reactions for what you do and say. You might find that you're not really acting autonomously in these relationships, but instead you're on autopilot and responding to past hurts more than current opportunities. If you are truly interested in developing richer and more fulfilling relationships with your family, talking to a professional is also well worth consideration.

Issue: Your family doesn't approve of your friends.

As discussed, sometimes the first warning that your friends are taking you down an unhealthy path is that other important people in your life don't approve of them. So try to be as objective as you can be, and invite your family's feedback without giving them the opportunity to gang up on you. If you're convinced that your family is merely being judge-y without having your best interests at heart, it's time to work on drawing more of a line of independence between you and the opinions of your family. It's quite a delicate balance, but most of us must do it eventually; it's a similar process to drawing adequate boundaries (discussed above.)

Issue: Your friends belittle or don't approve of your family.

Here it's important, again, to be as objective as possible. Might your friends be picking up on aspects of your family dynamic that truly are problematic? Might they have only your health, independence, and growth in mind? Of course, even if their gripes have merit, it's not always comfortable to hear your friends criticizing the family you can't do anything about. Simply tell them you're aware but that they don't make you feel any better by piling on. (If you happen to complain about your family a lot, they might think that they are being supportive.)

But if your friends seem to criticize your family for no reason, it may very well be something about them, like jealousy or irritability, that is running the show. Try to let your friends know in the moment, casually and simply, that you don't want to hear them railing on your parents or siblings. If it continues, it's worth having a larger talk.

Issue: Your dependence on your family is keeping you from moving forward with friendships.

The first thing you might ask yourself in this scenario is what is it that you are getting from your family that you are so afraid to try to get from other people. Do you think that only your family can know the real you? Or is it that you think the real you will be unlovable to others? One person's "I'm very close with my mom" is another person's significant psychological problem, so everyone has different thresholds for what they consider acceptable. But if you feel like you can't let anybody in because your family is the moat that keeps you protected, it might be time to do some serious searching about why that is. You might also start trying to climb out of your shell with some of the techniques from chapter 4.

Issue: Drama in your family is causing you to exhaust your friendships for support.

Many friendships have been wrecked by the constant complaining of one of the parties. The balance of reciprocity can easily be upset by the seventeenth repetition of "My sister is *such* a bitch!" And often, when the complaints revolve around family issues, the groans from the ever-listening friends are particularly pained because unlike with job or romantic relationship issues, it is usually not possible (without the help of the Witness Protection Program) to simply quit your family and start up with a new one. Making these challenges even more taxing, family problems most likely stem from dynamics that go all the way back to diapers and teddy bears, so they're even more deeply ingrained and devoid of easy solutions.

If you are the aggrieved friend, know your limits. Don't let your frustration build up to the point where you're going to explode— straws breaking the camel's back are rarely the soundtrack of a graceful exchange. If you are the friend doing the complaining, try to limit yourself a bit not just for your friends' sakes, but because there is a difference between venting and ruminating. Having the same complaints over and over again, without any attempt to change the problem, is probably not doing you any good, either.

Issue: You haven't yet gotten over issues with your family, and it spills into how you treat your friends and the quality of friendships that you have.

How perfect would it be if those people whose families left a lot to be desired in terms of their emotional health were able to automatically fill those holes with perfectly suited friends and seamlessly make the replacement? Unfortunately, this is rare. The more we lack from our families, the shakier our foundation is of knowing what we're supposed to be looking for in healthy relationships. If dinner with your parents always consisted of a heaping pile of yelling with the rigatoni, then you probably aren't the most practiced in holding down a peaceful, natural conversation. If your family constantly violated your privacy, betrayed your trust, or criticized your every move, then your expectations of how your friends should behave—and of what you deserve—will definitely be affected. It certainly doesn't mean you're doomed. But you must know your vulnerabilities and be vigilant against falling into similar patterns with your friends. Specifically, you need to give a bit more attention to the screening process of whom you let into your life and what kind of treatment you'll put up with. You'll also need to work harder to learn what makes up a functional relationship, and how to feel at ease in one.

Issue: Forget your family—it's your significant other's family drama that's making you crazy!

Where would marriage counselors be without the drama of in-laws? Ellie shares a classic example:

My husband's parents don't particularly like me, and have made it clear since I started dating him. So when they joined Facebook, they turned it into a competition. I would post a photo with my mom and a few days later we would hear about how we never mention them or don't communicate with them as much. I felt like I was being watched. Finally, my mother-in-law said that I upset her so much, it was giving her stomach issues, which in turn she feels will develop into cancer. It caused a huge extended family blowup. At that point, I defriended all my in-laws so I don't have to deal with them.

Ellie was able to take matters into her own hands and protect herself in the way that she needed. Generally, when your partner's family is giving you grief, it's also a reasonable expectation for your significant other to play the role of mediator. He or she should be able to intervene in ways that establish what is acceptable behavior. Of course, some families can still make people's lives miserable, but when you're in a partnership, you should never have to go it alone—or without some semblance of a shield.

As research makes it more and more clear that friendships can impact our health and happiness just as much as, if not more than, our families, it's important to look at the ways we can incorporate both into our daily lives harmoniously. The meaning that friends can have in the arc of our lives—despite or perhaps because of the fact that they're not with us from Day One—is something that can no longer be ignored. And by being more flexible about how we view the boundaries between friends and family, and being careful to deal with issues proactively as they arise, we're likely to enlarge our support network and enrich our life experiences more than we ever could have imagined.

10

WHEN FRIENDSHIPS GO SOUTH

Let's reiterate: Any friendship, at its core, is two people's connection at any one moment—or string of moments—in time. (Modern science has not yet figured out a way to have two people exist simultaneously in different time periods, since they're too busy making the iPhone smaller.) So it's unrealistic to expect that the person you were closest to at one point in your life will also be the person that you want by your side through every subsequent stage. And it's important to remember that if you have a wonderful relationship that eventually becomes less wonderful, the ending of the friendship should not negate the positive experiences that came before it. In short, sometimes friendships evaporate or even sour, and it's not always someone's fault.

Often, though, the difficulty comes from both people not being on the same page about the friendship's demise. Even more confusing is that it sometimes takes a conscious, proactive decision to end a friendship—and they don't exactly make Hallmark cards for that. Unequal expectations, breakdowns in communication, and generally icky feelings make the deterioration of friendships even harder to bear. Still worse, there's no cultural narrative or recognized rituals for the breaking up of a friendship—where's the *Divorce Court* for sparring BFFs?

Thus, friendships don't always end cleanly or quickly. The finale is often ambiguous, drawn out, and replete with all kinds of distress. Many times the lead-up to the breakup is fraught with indecision and confusion about why to do it, whether to do it, and how to do it. There are no hard-and-fast rules about whether to keep a friendship on life support, how long to put up with dissatisfaction, or how many second chances an erring friend deserves. Nonetheless, there are some clear signs that a friendship is in jeopardy.

5 WARNiNG SiGNS THAT A FRiENDSHiP IS STRUGGLiNG

In these cases, it's worth doing the emotional equivalent of a doctor's checkup:

1. You do not like the person you become when you're around that friend.

Maybe you feel passive-aggressive, or even downright aggressive, or you notice that you have a sharper edge to you. Perhaps you feel petty or jealous, or must admit that you don't really seem to want the best for your friend. This may manifest itself not just in regular flickers of jealousy but in an overarching feeling that you don't want her to succeed.

2. Your friend does not seem to appreciate the person you are.

You find yourself constantly embarrassed by how late you sleep or how big your feet are or the fact that you couldn't tell anise from arsenic. You feel underappreciated for your real self and have a nagging urge to cover up what you perceive to be your "flaws." (Or maybe you want to flaunt them aggressively in your friend's face, just to get some pleasure from getting on their nerves.) You're embarrassed when you say the wrong thing, or "screw up" something (which seems to happen a lot), or you have the nagging feeling that your friend seems to appreciate you only conditionally.

3. The words you would use to describe that friend are not flattering.

You find yourself dwelling on unfavorable characteristics or making fun of the person in your head. You feel condescension or resentment toward them, not just from one particular event, but in general. You're not laughing with them—you're laughing at them. Let's be honest: you just don't seem to like them anymore.

4. The friendship feels totally unbalanced.

You feel that reciprocity in your relationship has gradually been lost or was never there to begin with. This could be because you feel that you are pulling all the weight in the relationship. Other times, it's that someone is always trying to do so much for you, and you don't feel as interested in returning the favor; their kindness feels more like a burden than a gift.

5. Your friend is bringing out bad behaviors in you.

When you're around them, you drink a lot more, feel your creativity stifled, try too hard to conform, or perhaps you become more cruel or dishonest. Maybe there are more tangible markers, like your job or grades are more in jeopardy the more time you spend with this person. Either way, this reeks of "bad influence."

If you feel this way about all your friendships, you might be struggling with challenges that are greater than the individual relationships. See chapter 11 for thoughts about when talking to a therapist could be helpful. But if there's one particular relationship that hits all these markers, it's time to think about an endgame.

A MISMATCH? OR NATURAL DRIFTING APART?

Perfectly happy friendships may eventually develop cracks over time. And it's sometimes neither person's fault, just the natural effect of sheer circumstance—people grow at different rates. The question, when these cracks develop, is at what point to bother breaking out the spackle. When is it worth the effort to try to keep a friendship going, when you both seem to be drifting apart?

The first clues come from what might be responsible for the shifting dynamic. Is it external life circumstances, or something more internal? Chapter 7 discussed life transitions and how they can affect friendships, both superficially and profoundly. Other times, what is causing the drift—or a downright rift—is harder to put a finger on.

Is there still room for each of you in each other's lives? Do you still seem to relate to each other? Is there genuine affection there? Are you willing to put forth the effort to get through whatever stagnation has occurred?

HOW TO BREAK UP WHEN IT'S NOT YOU, IT'S THEM

Of the friendships that aren't built to survive the new challenge, some will break apart naturally. Other relationships, however, might require more work to end:

- **The Slow Fade:** Done right, this is usually one of the best ways to end a friendship. Maybe it's lessening the amount of responses you give to her, or lengthening the amount of time in between your contact. Maybe it's asking fewer questions or making a subtle point not to keep up as well with her daily life. But there's a fine line between this and . . .

- **The String-Along:** This is actually one of the cruelest ways to break up a friendship, and it's quite taxing for both of you. Your intentions might be off-the-charts good. That may even be what's getting you in trouble—they say the road to hell is paved with good intentions. (Of course, so is the road to a major bathroom remodeling, another version of hell.) You don't want to hurt their feelings, and you fear the discomfort that would come from being clearer in your intentions, so you string them along. Maybe you flake out on dinner several times in a row, you leave them in the lurch about whether you'll share the ski trip expenses, or you're inexcusably late to RSVP for their baby's baptism—when you've been named the godmother! You've crossed the line from subtle to aggressive, from gentle to gang-busters. Procrastination is bad enough without bringing someone else down with your ship. Don't leave them hanging—and don't string them along.

- **The Clean Break:** Direct and to the point, this lets the other person know that there's a fundamental disconnect in your lifestyles. This can sometimes be appropriate when what's ending your friendship appears to be a change in values, a change in priorities, or a feeling that they're going down a path that is not healthy for you. With a more general drifting apart, however, it might feel awkward or downright cruel to hammer home the point that you no longer foresee being a big part of each other's lives. So it's often a good option only when the Slow Fade hasn't gotten the hint across.
- **The Explosion:** This is sort of like the Clean Break, if a gigantic helping of lighter fluid were involved. It's generally not a good idea, and is often not done intentionally. It often follows a betrayal, an argument that got too personal, or a silent treatment that froze into an intractable ice cap.
- **The Sabotage:** This occurs when you do something awful in the hopes that your friend will be the one to end the friendship. But it's so cruel! It puts the onus of effort and hand-wringing on your friend. Why inflict anguish and guilt on a person when the general expectations and responsibilities of friendship dictate that you summon the

gumption to end things yourself? They have no idea that you're secretly urging them to pull the trigger—which you should buck up and do yourself, rather than hurting them until they've had enough and do it for you.

While these types of friendship breakups may appear to be clear-cut, real-life relationships are often messier than these categories can convey. A friendship breakup can be oodles more dramatic than even the most soap opera–esque of romantic bust-ups. And it might be a hybrid of several different types of breakups. Take this one, from Laurie:

We still work at the same company. I'm five years her senior and used to refer to her jokingly as "Mini-Me." She reminded me so much of myself at that age and all the issues/ awkwardness I had been dealing with. We became very close over several years, and much of our time was spent talking about how "different" we were from other people. I felt much like an older sister.

Then it became too close for comfort. I felt like she was siphoning off parts of my personality—almost taking over bits of my identity. We had a very routine social life, basically hanging out at the same two bars. I got pretty silent over e-mail to her; I told her I was in a bad mood in general. Then three days later, I got an e-mail from her, calling me a "hypocritical bitch" and saying the friendship was over. She claimed stake over one bar and told me I could have the other.

We tried to talk it out in person, but at one point, she turned away from me and started reading a magazine. It all collapsed from there. She dumped all the stuff she had borrowed from me out in the open at work. Threw my spare house keys in a bar. It was like the worst breakup I've ever had. People commented that it sounded like we were dating. I did get an apology e-mail from her months later, saying that she realized she handled it poorly and was hoping that we could say hi should we run into each other. That very day, we did run into each other, and she turned away when I waved and refused to make eye contact.

Now I get the occasional text out of the blue, telling me that it physically hurts her to see me and that she'd like to avoid it. I actually feel happier without her in my life. I feel bad saying that, but I view it as a toxic friendship, one that kept me mired in despair and fed all my fears and anxieties. I think it's better for both of us not to be friends, but I know she doesn't see it that way. She feels victimized and spurned.

Sometimes, the explosions can be so forceful so as to involve the federal government, as Zoe's did:

We were sorority sisters. We both ended up not finishing college, but she always sent birthday and Christmas cards. Seven or eight years after I left college, I moved into her new neighborhood, and we started seeing each other more. Then we both started planning our weddings, and then our husbands started hanging out; they sort of had a bromance going. But then I started seeing things as I got to know her better. She'd say cruel things about her "friends"—initially, it was kind of funny, but after a while, it wasn't. Eventually, my husband kind of outgrew her husband, too. He then got a better job and we needed to move. I was hoping that with us moving, the relationship would die a natural death. But out of the blue, we get this call for us to be interviewed for her security clearance. The guy's not there for very long. He asked very specific questions, and says, "Does she do any illegal drugs?"

Had she asked me in advance, I would have told her, "I know you smoke weed—are you sure you want to list me? Because I don't want to lie." But I truthfully told the guy, "I've never seen her do it." So, that went back and forth for a little bit. ("Do you know that she does it?" "I've never seen her.") Finally, my husband goes, "She wrote about it on her blog!" The guy asked how many blogs she had, and then concluded, "She's not a discreet person." He then asked me: "Would you trust her with a security clearance?" I said, "What level?" And he said it doesn't matter. I had to be honest. "Probably not." Then he left.

So eventually she e-mails me, "After ten years of friendship, regretfully, it's over." I was sort of confused. I said, "I'm sorry you feel this way, but perhaps our friendship ended the day you expected me to lie for you." And then there was barbing back and forth. She claimed that she had the transcript (but the guy didn't take notes and didn't have a tape recorder!) and that I said all these things I didn't. Then she blogged about it, using my initials and details. She painted me as this miserable, bitter failure. She was venomous and hateful. Other people who saw it came to my defense on her blog (which she accused me of doing) but then she deleted the blog completely. I think she was just afraid of legal repercussions—I don't see her being able to realize she behaved badly.

I was really hurt; I lost much sleep over it. We could've just moved away, let things fade out, and sent Christmas cards. The old neighborhood is such a painful reminder. When a friendship breaks with such trauma, it's sooo stressful and painful.

And sometimes, there are the friend breakups that begin with an embarrassing occurrence followed by piercing silence or a disappearing act. You might ask yourself how long to keep contacting the person and might finally give up. In the age of social networking, though, they just might pop back into your life and create new complexities years later. If you're the embarrassed one, the following story emphasizes the importance of addressing the issue once and for all in order to move forward. In a saga that involves complications from weddings, alcohol, and Facebook, Gwen explains:

My wedding reception was going so smoothly—and we were all having so much fun. I was talking to my bridesmaid Jenna; she was being so affectionate and we were all having such a great time together. But awhile later, another bridesmaid told me that Jenna was passed out drunk in the bathroom. When we found her, a security guard intervened and said we needed to get her back to her hotel. But she was too drunk to tell anyone where she was staying! (I knew she wasn't in the wedding hotel.) We're trying to rummage through her purse to find a room key; finally my wedding planner says she'll get her a cab and handle it. I thought everything was taken care of.

I found out when I came back from my honeymoon that another bridesmaid and her boyfriend had to drive her home because she was so incoherent in the cab that the driver felt uncomfortable and brought her back! I tried to contact her to ask if she made it back okay; I e-mailed and called, but it was like she totally dropped off the face of the planet. I asked around, and other people said they had contact with her all the time. This actually went on for a few years. Finally, I wrote her a letter: "If you're embarrassed, please don't worry about it. I just want to know that everything's okay." And once again, I never heard from her.

A full five years later, she friended me on Facebook. I

accepted it, like, *Here's my chance to finally find out what's going on.* I saw from her profile she's married; I wrote her a nice message about how I've missed her, asking how she's doing. I hoped we'd address the weirdness. She just responded, "Oh, I see you have a little boy!" It's like she just woke up and decided to pretend that the entire thing never happened. Often now, she'll comment on my Facebook status or make simple remarks here and there. It's such a weird thing, like she's trying to be involved in my life but not really. It's a really strange relationship.

MOVING ON

Because there are no culturally delineated rituals for ending friendships, people are often at a loss about whether what they're feeling is appropriate after a broken friendship. They sometimes feel silly or strange for going through a mourning period that's as sad and painful as—if not more than—that of a romantic relationship.

But try to remember that the pain you feel is validation of the meaning and connection you had with that person. As much as it is my hope that you can avoid explosive breakups, it's true that the occasional ending of a platonic relationship, and the sometimes searing misery and nagging sense of loss that accompany it, is often the price of allowing ourselves to love and trust other people.

Give yourself time. And don't feel you have to excuse your feelings. Many people that I talked to over the course of researching this book had a heartbreaking friendship that they identified as causing more turmoil than any of their romances—combined. It's not often talked about, but it should be. Don't compound your stress and sense of loss by telling yourself that you're not allowed to feel that way.

TAKING STOCK: WHAT YOU CAN LEARN FROM
ROAD-KiLLED RELATIONSHiPS

Another way to see the light at the end of a friendship-breakup tunnel is to use the experience to learn and grow. When a breakup is part of a larger pattern, you have an especially rich cache of data.

Make a list of the last few friendships that you consider lost and ask yourself the following questions about each person:

How would you describe that person, in reality?

How would you describe the vision of them that you were drawn to?

Did your view of them change over time? Or did they? Did you?

How long did your relationship last?

Who broke up with whom, and why?

Is someone at fault? Is it split between both of you? What percentage would you give each of you? Or is it no one's fault but sheer circumstance?

Do you regret it (the relationship itself, or the breakup)?

Maybe you won't find any overt patterns except for noting that your handwriting has gotten particularly bad. But often, by looking at the rap sheet of your relationship offenses and crashes, you'll be able to pick out a possible issue that not only pervades past relationships, but also might get in the way of future ones as well. Common stumbling blocks include the following:

Falling for Ms. Wrong

Do you always find a way to get close to drama queens? Do you fall for friends whom you think you can fix, but then they exploit you or bring you down with them? Are you drawn to the snarky gossipers who make you cackle with laughter about that girl in the cube next to yours, but then horrify you when you realize they're saying even worse about you? These issues all begin with your choices. Go back to chapter 2 and spend a little more time examining what kinds of qualities you should be seeking out instead of the ones that have lured you in.

Creating Firestorms of Drama in Your Relationships

Perhaps you are the one creating the drama. You might not have been honest with yourself about this until you really start examining your patterns. If you tend to do this, though, you're sabotaging not just your friendships but probably many other aspects of your life as well, including your work and your family relationships. The search for the root of it might be well served by help from a professional.

Fleeing a Relationship When It Is No Longer Convenient for You

Do you tend not to stick it out when the going gets rough? Do you pull the plug on not just your worst relationships but most of them at some point or another? If so, you might start examining what's realistic in terms of the reciprocity and effort involved in keeping up a friendship and whether you are taking advantage of others, or just being so passive that you let your friendships die on the vine when they could have had years of life left in them. Remind yourself of what true, deep friendship can bring to your emotional health and ask yourself why you're not willing to put in a bit of effort to make that happen.

Ditching Older Friends for Newer Upgrades

The stereotype of a businessman hunting for an arm candy second wife has grown pretty tired. But a similar phenomenon exists in platonic relationships. Just as you might have ditched your playmate since preschool (she still didn't wear a bra!) when you went to junior high and tried to get in with the cool crowd, so, too, exists the temptation to latch on to a newer, more sparkly adult friend who seems at first glance to outshine your old circle. You might also do this by social poaching; maybe you're leaving your friends for the more glittering people that they introduced you to.

But you do absolutely everyone involved a disservice in this case. You're probably not, in any of the friendships, getting to the point of reaping the benefits of a nourished, long-term, unconditional relationship. It's great to add new friends, but when they're appealing only as flashy new models, you're getting all style and no substance.

Being Unable to Bring Friendships to the Next Level

Perhaps you have a dozen friends who are all close . . . ish. They're more than acquaintances but less than anything else. So there's probably something making you afraid to let people in to a greater level of intimacy. One doesn't have to be alone to feel lonely. To deal, pay close attention to what was discussed in terms of making friends more like family (chapter 9) and "5 Ways to Make Good Friendships Greater" (chapter 6).

Choosing Fleeting Relationships by Circumstance

This is self-sabotage in its purest form. Just like the person whom we'd stereotypically brand a "commitment phobe" because he tends to fall for the person who's moving to Southeast Asia a month from now, so, too, can the platonic friend-seeker choose nothing but temporary prospects.

Having So Many Friendships That You Can't Keep Up

This Jill-of-all-trades, mistress-of-none approach can sometimes make someone look like they have the best friendships in the world. They're outgoing, they're popular, and if they want to throw a barbecue, they can have a houseful of people within two hours clamoring to line up in front of the pickle relish. But if you look closer, a troubling pattern emerges—none of these friendships is particularly long lasting, and there lies a wake of people who have gradually gotten fed up with, or been forgotten by, the Star of the Show. It's not uncommon for someone to try to please so many people that they acquire friend after friend, making promise after promise. Gradually, they might begin to realize that there is a huge crowd of people that they never got back to about getting together, or whom they completely dropped the ball on in some more serious way.

Quality trumps quantity. It's hard to remember this in the days of collecting friends like Pokémon cards on social networking sites, but little good does the huge invite list do you if none of those people will still be in your circle next year. Like having so many dates that you accidentally start calling them by each other's names, if you're trying to fill your days with too much socialization and juggling too many people, the balls are eventually going to come crashing down.

Being Sucked into a Honeymoon Period of Friendship, Then Coming to Reality

Maybe you rush into friendships with all the fervor of a rabid, pennant-waving fan, putting your new BFFs on a pedestal and developing platonic crushes whose energy and intensity could light the night sky. You can't stop talking about these new friends, and you push things to move quickly. You're smitten with the idea of them but are bound to crash down to earth when you realize that there are aspects of them that aren't perfectly compatible with you, or that you don't even like very much.

In a cruel paradox, this is most likely to happen when you are feeling lonely. The more you want to find that perfect friend, the more likely you are to latch on to the idea of a friendship before the real foundation of it has a chance to gel and develop. Don't put all your eggs in one basket. If this is a pattern for you, you've got to learn to, shall we say, curb your enthusiasm (!) a bit. Give things more time and diversify your options.

Blaming and Turning On Others; Just Wanting to Be Alone

Do you tend to get resentful of virtually all your friends after a certain amount of time? Do you get tired of people and start to push them away out of antsiness, boredom, or discomfort? Several issues could be at work here, whether you just have a more mild and drawn-out honeymoon phase, you avoid conflict to the point that lingering tensions eventually break the camel's back, or you start to feel uncomfortable with the power that someone has from knowing you too well. Often, this is a problem with intimacy and trust, which might be professionally explored. Or perhaps you are a quieter person who enjoys more alone time than you're acknowledging, and in the meantime you're letting your friends prevent you from getting that.

Focusing on the patterns that you've developed in your relationships is one of the best ways to learn from what's hurt you. No one can guarantee that you won't have a doozy of a friendship breakup in the future—and it very well might hurt. But the more you know about yourself and what your needs are, the better able you are not only to avoid traveling that path, but also to come out of it stronger and more insightful if it does happen.

11

WHEN IT'S SOMETHING MORE SERIOUS:

Psych Issues, Bad Patterns, and Getting More Help

It's simple: When someone is in the throes of a depression, attending to his or her friendships can become quite difficult. When the world seems so dark that it feels arduous to get out of bed in the morning or pay your phone bill, how can you possibly keep up your patient enthusiasm for listening to your friend jabber on about her views about the character development in *Gossip Girl*?

COMMON PSYCHOLOGICAL PROBLEMS THAT CAN POISON RELATIONSHIPS

This is a common crossroads. About 7 percent of American adults suffer from clinical depression in any given year,[1] and the numbers appear to be climbing. The symptoms of depression often first show up by making someone a very different kind of friend—usually much worse—than they used to be. And so their friends feel wronged and might feel personally slighted. They might think that their friendship is cooling off, or that their friend is becoming

---

[1] *Archives of General Psychiatry*, 2005 June; 62(6): 617–627.

boring or preoccupied, or even that she's turning into a first-class bee-yotch. It's understandable to get completely irritated when you've been bailed on for sushi for the fourth time. (You really wanted those Philadelphia rolls!) But before you start diagnosing it as a problem within the friendship, it's important to remember that it could be a much more serious problem with your friend herself. The following are common signs and symptoms of depression:[2]

- Feelings of hopelessness, worthlessness, or excessive guilt
- Feeling taxed by the simplest of mental activities (indecision, not being able to concentrate, feeling "mentally exhausted")
- Not finding pleasure in activities that used to bring joy (or not participating in things like they used to)
- Shifts in sleeping (no longer sleeping much, or sleeping much more than usual)
- Changes in eating (loss of appetite and/or dropping weight unintentionally, or eating more than usual and putting on weight)
- Irritability
- Sadness

Notice that what we most commonly think of as depression—sadness—is only one of the many symptoms of the actual clinical disorder of depression. In real life, these clinical symptoms often manifest themselves as—let's be honest—making someone a bummer to be around. While someone used to be curious, they are now subdued. While someone used to be ready to chuckle, they are now quiet. While someone used to be known for being willing

---

[2] American Psychiatric Association, *Diagnostic and Statistical Manual of Mental Disorders: DSM-IV* (Washington, D.C.: APA, 1994.)

to ringlead a random trip to a karaoke bar at 10 P.M. on a Tuesday, they now would rather stay in every night of the week.

It's easy to get defensive when all of a sudden a friend of yours is less responsive, more irritable, more negative, and less receptive to listening to your sixth recounting of that cell phone customer service nightmare. But there is no other time when the need for a good, solid friendship is as dire as when someone is struggling with a mental health issue like depression. While the most understandable temptation might be to get annoyed and let the friendship fade, resisting that impulse is one of the most important roles you can play in someone's life: giving them a lifeline when they are struggling with a black hole closing in.

It's not just about depression. Although it's the most common mental health issue to strike young adults, it's certainly not the only one. Anxiety disorders of all shapes and sizes are also quite ubiquitous. Chances are, either you or a person within a few yards of you at the coffee shop right this very moment is suffering from problems with anxiety. (And no, it's not just the espresso.)

In many ways, these problems can mimic the symptoms of depression. Depression and anxiety can be intricately interwoven. With anxiety, you'll often see a heightened sense of edginess or irritability. Sometimes this manifests in negativity. ("Who is this idiot that's always on this detergent commercial?" "What do you mean you're stuck in traffic? You should've taken the boulevard!") Or, like depression, it can also lead to pessimism. ("There's no way I'll get that job." "I'm so not a fan of those jeans on you.") The person might be less patient and just generally seem more bothered. They often seem more fearful, turning down various activities, or overly judgmental about other people.

Another type of anxiety disorder is posttraumatic stress disorder. PTSD, while recently in the news for its devastating effect on many troops returning from war zones, can strike anyone who's experienced something horrifying. Certainly not everyone who's been through a trauma will go on to experience the symptoms of PTSD, but many will. And whether that trauma is a car accident, an assault, watching someone else get seriously injured, or a natural disaster, PTSD can interfere significantly in their ability to move on afterwards.

If someone has experienced a trauma, you can best be a friend to them by encouraging them to talk about it at their own pace and get help. They might be tempted to isolate themselves and shut down, but that can sometimes prohibit them from getting the help they need to heal. In fact, social support, as discussed in the introduction, actually improves the prognosis for PTSD.

Eating disorders are also extremely common among young American women. Though the range and variation of disordered eating patterns are beyond the scope of this book, when you are concerned about someone's eating, exercise habits, attitude about their body or size, or significant changes in their weight, it's important to tread carefully. Many people take the immediate tactic of focusing in on what they perceive to be the problem: "You eat too little." "You're too skinny." "You've got to stop exercising so much." In reality, if the person does have an eating disorder, these interventions can do more harm than good, as they once again focus the attention on how the person looks or what they eat. For people suffering from eating and body image problems, that's already the big problem: They define themselves by these external factors and think they're the only things that matter. Your accentuating that point only reinforces that idea. Instead, try emphasizing how you're concerned that they seem unhappy, stressed, tired, or different from their usual selves, and try to get a dialogue going. You must underscore, at all costs, that it is the real person whom you love and care about, and that you're not going to be fooled by outside appearances being indicative of who they are underneath.

It's also important to remember that some of these behaviors and attitudes can be catching. If you have a friend who is struggling with problems with eating or body image, as much as you should be involved in helping her seek help, please do keep an eye on your own thoughts and patterns as well.

WHAT *NOT* TO SAY WHEN SOMEONE'S EXPERIENCED A LOSS

A common issue that can produce friction in friendships is not knowing what to say when someone has experienced a loss. Whether it is a miscarriage, the death of a loved one, or even a painful divorce, sometimes the worst mistake a friend can make is being so scared of not knowing what to say that they just disappear. With that in mind, here's a hint: Just be there and try your best. For those of you terrified of saying the wrong thing, here's a cheat sheet:

"I know how you feel." Honestly, you don't, you won't, and you can't. Even if you've gone through what seems to be the exact situation, there's no way that the conditions, and your psychological makeup and reactions, could be similar enough to your friend's for you to truly understand exactly how your friend feels. But that shouldn't stop you from offering your empathy, or talking about how you relate to her. Just be wary of acting like you can get inside their head—you'll come off as a know-it-all who's less interested in talking about them than in yourself.

"This, too, shall pass." Though a good phrase for cross-stitching into a throw pillow (or repeating to yourself when you're having the kind of day where hitting your thumb with a hammer would be an improvement), this is rarely helpful for someone in the throes of a loss. At that moment in time, the person doesn't feel like their pain will ever pass. And though it would indeed be helpful for them eventually to realize it will, your simply declaring it so won't make them believe it; they need more time.

"This is God's plan." This can be confusing, unhelpful or, in a worst-case scenario, enraging. ("Why does God think I deserve this?") If you know for certain that you and your friend share the same faith, then certainly, gently nudge them toward a reminder of their beliefs. But don't act like you have the master plan of their life all figured out, especially when they may feel like nothing makes sense anymore.

"If you need anything, give me a call." This is no doubt well meaning, and it's the calling card of friends helping grieving friends the world over. But it's too general, and it puts the burden of effort onto the individual who's in pain. It's sort of like giving the gift of extra work (intimately familiar to anyone who's ever been presented with a ribbon-wrapped exotic plant or sourdough starter). Often, when someone is experiencing the emotional paralysis that comes with grieving, the last thing they feel like doing is initiating asking someone for help. This is especially true for people who have trouble asking for help in the first place. They don't want to put anyone out, and it's difficult to take advantage of the "just ask" invitation when it's become such a common cliché. Yes, your friend would love not to have to deal with finding something for dinner when they've been crying for the past couple of hours, but they certainly don't feel comfortable asking you to go grab takeout. So why not take the initiative to call and ask if you can drop it by? Yes, she would love to have someone to be with as a distraction on Sunday morning when she's feeling down, but she doesn't want to bother you or intrude on your life, so why not gently let her know that you really want to take her to breakfast and suggest a couple of dates?

If only there were a limit to the difficult issues that can develop over someone's lifetime. But it's quite possible that you've already been personally affected not only by these issues, but by a host of other problems as well. Being concerned with a friend's drinking or drug use, relationship violence, cutting behavior, sexual recklessness, financial irresponsibility, or legal self-destruction is a far too common situation. The good news is that the path toward encouraging someone to get help is many times very similar, no matter the intricacies of the specific challenge being faced. In all these situations of emotional difficulty, encouraging the person to seek proper help—usually in the form of mental health assessment and treatment—is one of the most important things you can do. Many people have a discomfort or unfamiliarity with therapy, so they feel weird suggesting it to someone else. You might also feel that suggesting they need to talk to a professional is pushing that person away, making it sound like you don't want to listen anymore. Still others feel like it will make their friend think that they're saying that they're crazy. The rest of this chapter is devoted to helping make that process more comfortable.

WHEN SOMETHING'S NOT RIGHT: HOW TO HELP A FRIEND IN TROUBLE

So how do you suggest professional mental health help when you've never had it yourself? How can you convince someone that therapy can be beneficial when you're not even sure how it works?

First, try to convey to your friend that her issues are real, common, and treatable. The "real" part is important because too many other people might just be telling her that she needs to "get over it," or she herself might be thinking that she just needs to be happy. Maybe she feels like she's complaining over nothing. It's your job to validate to her that depression, or any of the other challenges mentioned, is a disorder like any physical one. It is *not* "all in her head." (Or I guess it is, in the same way that the pain you feel when I put a needle through your big toe is also, technically, all in your head.)

The "common" part is also important. It's not to make your friend think that it's no big deal or that she's not unique, but it's to give her hope that other people have gone through this and have come out the other side. She needs the assurance that right there in her very own city are therapists who have seen this and know how to handle it, and that millions of dollars have been spent on developing medications that might also help bring relief.

This leads us to the final part of the message of "real, common, and treatable"—yes, it's treatable. You might not know the first thing about psychology or depression. You might think that Freud was a rock band. But you can still be instrumental in conveying a message of hope to your friend, armed with just the knowledge in this chapter.

Offer her logistical help as well—poring through her insurance plan, looking at psychologists' profiles, calling for availability, and even accompanying her to the appointment (though you'll understandably need to stay in the waiting room). Often, when someone's mental health is struggling, one of the first factors to be affected is the wherewithal to take care of details. It can be excruciatingly hard just to compile some phone numbers or leave some messages. That's something you can help with. There can also be considerable trepidation about taking that first step and actually going—which is why your car, or your gentle presence on the bus, cab, or subway, can work wonders.

Most of all, give your friend a sense of hope: that you believe in her ability to feel better, and that you are willing to be beside her through the process to get there.

WARNING SIGNS THAT MORE IMMEDIATE HELP IS NEEDED

Sometimes, there are signs that help is needed in an even more urgent manner. In these instances, it's even more important not to put off talking to your friend and seeing that they get connected to help.

Talking about suicide. It seems obvious that when someone mentions the idea of killing themselves or ending their lives a good friend would pay attention. But that kind of talk is so commonly used in jest (note: it's an awful idea to use "I'll open a vein" as slang!) that many people are lured into a false sense of security and start to ignore their friends' cries for help. Of course there's a chance that your friend is completely (and inappropriately) joking. But there's also a chance that they're using that "joke" as an opportunity to put their thoughts out there, either to vent their frustration and hopelessness or to test if anyone seems to care.

Making plans. When someone has gotten to the point of being specific about a method in their comments or is compiling the means to hurt themselves or end their lives, that is a warning sign that things have gotten more serious. Moreover, when someone has attempted suicide in the past, that's a sign that there may not be much of a barrier to them trying again.

Increased risk taking, substance abuse, or self-destructive behavior. Not only can this be a sign of increasing lack of concern about their safety and their life, but it can also physically make them that much more likely to injure themselves, intentionally or not.

Disciplinary, legal, or financial crises that bring about desperation. These can serve as both cause and effect when someone is in a bad place mentally.

An attempt to get affairs in order or give things away. This can be a sign that someone is anticipating that they won't be around anymore.

And there is one additional warning: Sometimes when someone is rebounding upward, they are at their most vulnerable. It's all too common that people are shocked when a loved one takes their own life, saying, "He seemed to be doing so much better!" But it's a cruel reality that when someone appears to be on the upswing from a deep depression, they can be particularly vulnerable to suicide. There are two main reasons for this: First, in the throes of a severe depression, a person may lack the energy to put together a logistical plan to end their lives. When they start to feel a bit better, they may gain some of that energy, and yet the bulk of the dark, hopeless thoughts may remain, making them more likely to put their plan into action.

The second reason is that some people may exhibit a resignation that appears as calmness once they have determined that they are going to end their lives. Friends might take this as a newfound happiness, when in reality it's a newfound determination to end their suffering through any means necessary.

How to Intervene in an Emergency

- Encourage the person to seek treatment, and convey the seriousness and depth of your concern.
- Stay with the person. Don't leave alone someone who you worry is at risk of harming themselves.
- Consider asking for immediate extra help by contacting additional friends, family, and the person's health care provider (if applicable).
- Don't be afraid to ask direct questions to find out how dire the scenario is, and again, to convey that there is help.
- Notify the authorities if there is an imminent concern.
- Consider calling a suicide prevention hotline for further support and guidance. 1-800-SUICIDE and 1-800-273-TALK are good places to start.

WHEN IT'S *YOU* STRUGGLING: HANGING ON TO YOUR FRIENDSHIPS WHEN YOU'D RATHER IGNORE THEIR CALLS

It's likely that at some point, it won't just be our friends who struggle with life's challenges, but we ourselves. And you might feel the urge to isolate yourself from your friends. Here's how to fight that instinct when friendships are sorely needed:

Let your friends give what they can. Try your hardest not to push them away, even if they're not always saying the right thing. Let them know what you need, if possible. Realize that they might think they're being shunned, so even if you don't want to talk, try to encourage their effort. "I really don't want to talk about it yet, but I appreciate that you're thinking of me."

Trust them to see the real you. Often we think that our friends, even our closest ones, might be horrified or judgmental to hear that we think we're depressed or have some other issue going on. In reality, a true friend will be relieved that you have opened up and want to help you get better in any way they can.

If you can stand it, ask for specific help. Maybe they can call your insurance company to help decode your coverage. Maybe they can get you out of that social obligation or even just bring a hot meal. Giving them specific tasks can often be helpful for both of you.

Remember the benefits of social support. Don't get trapped in the vicious circle of making yourself more miserable, more alone, and with less access to help by cutting yourself off from those who care about you.

Don't expect them to understand exactly, but trust them to care. You might not even understand what you're feeling yourself; it might be virtually impossible to put into words. Don't force it, and don't force them to get it. Know that their love for you is valuable in itself.

Try to think about getting better, for their sakes. But know that in the end, you must do it for yourself. Maybe you want them to stop worrying about you; you can use this as motivation to get you in the door of help. But part of getting better is realizing that you need to feel better not because you owe it to anyone else, but because it's what you deserve.

Be aware of contagion effects. This isn't to make you feel guilty, but it's food for thought: Sometimes problems like eating disorders, substance abuse, and even mood disorders can travel in packs. Getting help yourself can do your friends an even bigger favor by lowering their risk.

I PROMISE WE DON'T ALL HAVE WHITE BEARDS: HOW THERAPY CAN HELP

There are as many different types of psychotherapy, or talk therapy, as there are knitting techniques. (Trust me. I know both, and intimately.) And a large percentage of people who utilize it—and are helped by it—aren't even diagnosable with a specific psychological disorder so much as they are going through a challenging time or wanting to gain insight into themselves. If you recognized yourself in any of the previous chapters' discussions about bad relationship patterns, perhaps you might consider talking those through with a therapist, even if you feel pretty good. Learning about yourself is rarely a bad thing!

When you are looking for a therapist, the key is to be able to articulate what you're hoping to gain, not only so that you will know the type of therapy that corresponds best to what you need, but also so that you can convey that as clearly as possible to the potential therapists whom you talk to.

Among the most common types of modern psychotherapy are *cognitive-behavioral therapy (CBT)* and *psychodynamic psychotherapy.* CBT is a structured, empirically validated treatment that is more likely to be short-term and focused on relieving the symptoms that plague you, rather than making it a goal to delve extremely deep into their long-ago roots and causes. There might be set procedures for each session, possibly involving charting your progress or problems in some quantifiable way. Tangible homework assignments can be part of the process, and the idea is to scientifically unlock connections among thoughts, emotions, and behaviors. The therapist will often be direct and highly participatory in the sessions, challenging you like an investigator if you show signs of dysfunctional thought patterns. CBT is the darling of insurance companies because it is often short-term and very structured. It can be highly useful for certain disorders that are to-the-point: for instance, a phobia of spiders, a self-defeating pattern of pessimism, or social anxiety.

Psychodynamic psychotherapy is less cut-and-dried than CBT in terms of structure and duration. It focuses more on uncovering unconscious thoughts and feelings that are hindering you in your interactions and relationships, and it is not afraid to dig deep and delve into family history. Naturally, there is some overlap with CBT, though psychodynamic psychotherapists generally are less likely to use quantitative assessment techniques or tangible homework. But indeed, many modern therapists call themselves integrationists or "eclectic" in their orientations, offering a blend of several techniques (including many others than the two mentioned). And the blend—taking the best from all orientations and ideally suiting their style to the client at hand—can often work best. Regardless, the majority of individual therapy sessions are forty-five to fifty minutes long and meet on a weekly basis.

Some other considerations when finding a therapist:

1. Absolutely, the person should be licensed on a state level, whether they are a Ph.D. or Psy.D. psychologist, an MSW or LCSW social worker, or an M.A.-level counselor

(who generally have the shortest graduate training). Psychiatrists—identified by their M.D.—often only prescribe medication, though some do offer therapy.

2. If your insurance coverage is lacking or you do not feel you have the resources to pay for therapy, there are still many options available. Community mental health centers, nonprofit counseling centers, EAPs, psychologists who work on a sliding scale basis, and graduate school training programs all offer greatly reduced fees.

And a final word on therapy versus medication: It is my strong belief—and this is where I get to remind you of the fancy letters after my name—that no one should be on any kind of medication for mental health issues without also being under the care of a mental health professional. At the very least, this means you have frequent (every other week, or monthly at minimum) check-ins with a real-life human being. Otherwise, you run the risk of just putting a Band-Aid on the problem and denying yourself the tools to handle a future occurrence once you're off the medication. It's hard to gain the self-reliance, growth, and sense of autonomy that comes from feeling like you overcame a challenge when you're just popping a pill. It's also important to have a professional to help keep an eye on possible side effects of your medication.

There is also group therapy. As much as your late-night bitch sessions with your closest confidantes might feel like therapy, group therapy itself is a totally different beast, and it actually works best when you do not necessarily have any kind of relationship with the other participants outside of it. Group therapy varies from support groups where people are struggling with a specific issue in common to a more diverse group of people working together with a variety of challenges. It can be immensely helpful for people whose challenges stem from their relationship patterns.

With all of this talk about helping your troubled friends, there is sometimes a point at which it might be time to let go. I'm not advocating abandoning anyone when they're in danger. But there's a difference between being a true friend by helping someone through a rough patch and finding out that your friend's issues are indicative of a deepening and perhaps irreparable incompatibility. Often, we can overlook some unhealthy traits and behaviors early on, but when they start to wear thin, it becomes clear that merely standing by our friends might not do the trick. Know your limits. At some point, you have to protect yourself and end your stress, even though the guilt may live on. From Rayanne:

Through college, my best friend and I were inseparable. Honestly, I always knew she was a little troubled. She had lots of body and eating issues and pretty bad self-esteem with boys. She was really beautiful, but she let guys treat her like crap and was always interested in awful men. But there are lots of people who do stupid things in college—and during those years it didn't really affect our friendship. After college, I thought some of those issues would get better—and they just didn't. We were living a few hours apart, and she continued these awful dating patterns and eating issues, and was a chain-smoker. It's hard to admit, but I started disliking her. When she was a friend, she was one of the best I'd ever had. I knew she really cared about me; we'd have so much fun together when she put all this stuff aside. But the way she lived her life was really upsetting. And I found myself more and more like, "You really shouldn't be doing this to your body. You need to get help. You really shouldn't date this guy anymore," and I'd feel like a nagging bitch. And then she got an assignment in my city, so she started visiting a lot for work. I thought it would be a good thing, that we would do more regular, normal hanging out, instead of me always finding out new things at each visit and being appalled. But it got even worse because she started sleeping with one of her married-with-children bosses. So then I was in total nag mode. I couldn't control myself. And she'd ditch me at the last minute because he was able to slip away from his wife, all the while being ultra-possessive of me and jealous of my friends. It became more and more of a disaster, and I really just didn't like her anymore. She didn't even feel like my friend anymore, but it did feel like I was losing something that had been part of my life. She decided to move here permanently and was really excited. A week after she moved, I said, "I can't be friends when you're doing these things." Needless to say, she didn't take that well. We had a really, really mean phone conversation.

I lived in fear of running into her. It's been a few years, but to this day if I see anyone who looks like her walking down the street, I turn around and go the other way. I've tried to find out over the years what's happened to her, but no one's heard from her. I admit I Googled her, and she seems to have fallen off the face of the earth. I think I drew out the whole friendship breakup for longer than I needed to. I couldn't take it anymore, but I didn't know how to end it. I do feel guilty about it. If I see it from her perspective: "Oh, I'm finally moving where my best friend lives and am in a happy relationship with a guy . . . why doesn't she want to talk to me again?" She had, like, three therapists and was on lots of meds. She's just not a healthy person. In my fantasy for her, maybe that guy really was in love with her, and he eventually stayed with her and got her help with her issues. Maybe she's really happy, and things worked out. But I couldn't be a part of it anymore, though I still feel guilty. I tried my best, but in the end had to do what was right for me.

Perhaps there's no better summary for how to handle a friend who is struggling with significant issues: You owe it to them, yourself, and your history to try your best to help them. But you can't erase your own mental health from the equation. When patterns get entrenched, and the stress you're enduring on their behalf becomes a default and seemingly permanent pattern rather than a discrete time of crisis that you're helping them ride through, it's time to remember that it is only your life that you are truly responsible for. And in the end, you have to do what is right for you.

12

MAKING REAL FRIENDSHIPS A PRIORITY IN CHANGING TIMES

There's no doubt that some of the juiciest stories you could ever read are about what goes wrong in relationships. And certainly, there's much to be learned from those, as I hope you've seen. But the stories in our lives that matter most—what sustains us, enlivens us, and becomes our legacy—are not the drama of what went wrong. They're the connections that went so right.

STORIES FROM THE HEART OF FRIENDSHIP

From Katherine Chretian, a physician:

Anna was the "new girl" in eighth grade. I saw her, looking lost and unsure of herself, and took it upon myself to be her unofficial welcoming committee. We became friends instantly, soon talking late into the night during sleepovers and finding the joy in getting to know a person you are inexplicably drawn to. We confided our dreams to each other, our loves, our greatest fears. After we left to attend our respective colleges, we would still get together on breaks, and we quickly established a tradition of making simultaneous wishes on the first bite of our shared dessert. Throughout the years, we've weathered parental divorce, heartbreak, depression—and celebrated career changes, finding true love, and childbirth. Unlike many other friendships that have withered with distance, my friendship with Anna after twenty-two years remains strong, despite living on different continents. She has made my life more beautiful in so many ways—her romantic view of the world, her generous, gentle soul, her belief in me as a person, her love and undying friendship—and has undoubtedly shaped the woman I have become. My reward for befriending the "new girl" is more than I ever imagined. My world is more beautiful with Anna in it, and I love her for it.

From Kerry Gastley, a photographer:

I met Crystal as a child in 1979 when my family moved to her town in Georgia. We were great friends from the start. I remember vividly Crystal stapling her finger with the stapler—and I caught myself grasping my hand as if I had hurt my own hand. She was my best friend when my father was killed, when I was eleven. She never told me it was going to be okay like other people tried to do; she just let me cry and do whatever I felt like doing. I didn't have to be strong and keep it together. We were friends through going to different schools and even through her parents' divorce. She then moved off to Seattle. We finally got in touch again in the late '90s and Crystal came to visit me—it was as if time hadn't passed and we had been friends the whole time. It's always like that now, no matter how much time goes by. I know I can always depend on her—she really has been the one constant in my life. One year, we visited the graveyard where my father was buried and Crystal's grandfather (whom I had known and been very fond of) was buried as well. We weren't sure where the respective graves were, but we decided to get to the general area and just park and walk around, it was such a beau-

tiful day. We got out of the car and there was my dad's grave—and not far from that was her grandfather's grave! The funniest part of this is they were buried years apart. And the fact that their graves were so close to each other is quite amazing in a national cemetery—sort of like a sign. I see her as being a part of my life forever. Truly, always. Our next endeavor? A triathlon together next year.

From D'Arcey Johnson, an office manager:

Honestly, I cannot imagine my life without my two best friends. Other friends have come and gone over the years, but Kari and Amy and I will be celebrating our twenty-year "anniversary" next year. I met them when my family moved to town in fifth grade. Over two decades, we have been through so much together: guys, marriages, divorces, abusive relationships, passing of family members, infidelity. Fabulous new jobs and bosses from hell. The birth of children and the struggle for them. The dramatic implosion of my family, trips to Vegas and the beach and everywhere in between, triumphant graduations, vacations, and holidays. Whenever I encounter a bump in the road, they are always the first people I call, and likewise I am a lifeline to them. We survive it all together. We are each other's sounding boards for ideas great and small, and are always good for a word of advice, a laugh, or shoulder to cry on—and no small amount of sanity. We make it a point to schedule girls' weekends a couple of times a year, and we always try to get together to celebrate Christmas. Now that life is starting to interfere with what used to be effortless, I cherish these opportunities that much more. The notion of "Best Friends Forever" seems so, well, fifth grade—but in our case, it's true. Amy and Kari will always be a part of my life. Our kids will grow up with two additional aunts to love them, and, with hope, cousins and friends aplenty in each other. We have so many more places to go and things to experience! We've been through too much together to have anything stop us. I look forward to growing old with them and sharing the stories of our lifelong friendship with our kids and grandkids, complete with embarrassing photos, of course.

IT'S TRUE: FRIENDS REALLY DO MAKE YOU HAPPIER, HEALTHIER, AND PERHAPS EVEN SMARTER AND RICHER!

It's certainly possible to go through the next months and years of your life making no improvements in your friendships. The earth won't come crashing down. You won't turn purple. You'll still probably sleep and eat and get a laugh every now and then; life will proceed as usual. But if you're feeling lonely, disconnected, or overwhelmed and unsatisfied by your friendships—or even just vaguely unsupported in your life—why proceed as usual? There's magic to be had. So much of what we learn, in small ways and big ones, comes from others. And the human capacity to love and laugh in the company of other people is transcendent.

For those of you who need more tangible proof—yes, having strong relationships can make you physically healthier, too. And more emotionally stable and resilient. And, arguably, more responsible. More empathetic. More satisfied in life. More patient. More fulfilled. And yes, even richer.

4 SIMPLE THINGS YOU CAN DO TOMORROW (OR TONIGHT, IF YOU'RE FEELING GUNG-HO)

Maybe after reading all these stories, you're feeling inspired but stuck. Maybe you don't know where to begin. Maybe you feel like the issue is a lost cause. (Maybe you just flipped to this last chapter and are looking for a CliffsNotes guide to improving your relationships, pronto. Well, don't say I never gave you anything.)

1. Return that e-mail.

You know, the one that's been languishing in your in-box for weeks and makes you feel guilty every time you look (or try not to look) at it. Presuming it's someone you want to keep up a friendship with, what are you waiting for? You might feel that too much time has elapsed or that you've already screwed up, but that's all-or-none thinking that discounts the fact that there's a worthwhile friendship there, and that replying tomorrow is far better than replying two months from now, or not at all.

2. Plan a party for no reason.

It's absolutely fine if you're not Martha Stewart. This isn't about turning into Ms. Happy Hostess. You need not own an apron or margarita glasses, and you don't have to buy them, if that's not who you are. Anyone can make a brunch reservation, gather a group for a movie, get out some craft supplies, fire up the grill, order Chinese takeout, or get the hula hoops or Trivial Pursuit out of storage—whatever it takes. Take a handful of people (five to seven is a good number) that you like spending time with, and invite them to something. You might not even be the initiating type, but this is an opportunity to break out of your shell and take charge of keeping the people you care about close to you. If you genuinely enjoy spending time with these people, why not give yourself the power to make that happen more often?

3. Do a random, kind thing for one of your friends.

Maybe it's a goofy card in the mail (yes, the real mail!) or a candy bar left on their desk. Or just printing out a cute photo of the two of you—yes, make sure it is ultra-flattering of her—and putting it in a fun, funky frame. The small, sweet surprises in life are often what determine how well the days and weeks go.

4. Reach out and join something.

Maybe you're realizing that you don't actually have the friend to leave candy for or to invite to the barbecue. Or perhaps it's dawning on you that the only e-mails you have left unreturned were the ones inquiring not-so-subtly about the "size of your manhood." Maybe the problem isn't whom you know, but whom you don't know. If so, it's time to take a small but significant step toward connecting. Shoot off an e-mail to the head of an organization that interests you for volunteer or membership opportunities, and go back to chapter 4 to scour the list of other possibilities for connecting.

EXCUSES TO NiP iN THE BUD RiGHT NOW

I'm too busy. With what? It's about prioritizing. And few things matter more in life than the meaningful connections that we make with other people.

My friends are good enough. You picked up this book for a reason (besides the bribe—Hush!). It's easy to go with the inertia of assuming that nothing needs changing, but if you made it this far, you know in your heart that some friendships could use touch-ups. And you can always connect more: Let's say your friendships are indeed fine. Why not revel in that fineness—and guarantee it'll keep going—by scheduling some bonding time or writing a little "Thanks for being so awesome" note?

I'm too shy. I never claimed it would be easy-breezy to meet new people or strengthen the relationships you have. But reread the tips on branching out. It will be so, so worth it.

So what are you waiting for? Ultimately, our relationships with others are at the heart of what living is all about. They help us find meaning in our existence. They show us what love is, help us find laughter in the circumstances of our lives, and open us up to new experiences in ways that nothing else could do. There are infinite ways that we can be touched by other people and infinite types of friendships that will work together to shape the trajectory of our lives. Anyone who has been to a funeral has the point driven home to them through their sadness: Our biggest impact on this Earth is how we connect to other people and what we mean to them. By aligning ourselves with good people, and doing what we can to nourish those relationships, we add depth and breadth to our lives.

And there's evidence that we actually extend our lives and improve our health, too. We maximize our resources by having strong social support. From our mental health to our physical fitness, from our tangible, material resources to our intellectual development, it's our friends who in large part determine what we have to work with when we face the day.

DON'T JUST SIT THERE: GO OUT AND FRIEND AWAY!

You may have a thousand things to do tomorrow, or you may have skipped to these last pages without reading about the hows and whys of improving your relationships. Or you might feel that you don't know where to start. There's always a reason to put off making our connections greater, just as it always feels like there'll be a better time to start flossing, eating better, or spending more time outdoors. But by deciding to start, even in a small way, to repair a broken friendship, initiate a new one, or strengthen one that's at a crossroads, we're choosing to add meaning to our lives and to really start living.

That's so much more exciting than flossing. Why put it off?